Columbus and
the New World

American University Studies

Series IX
History

Vol. 185

PETER LANG
New York • Washington, D.C./Baltimore • Boston
Bern • Frankfurt am Main • Berlin • Vienna • Paris

Columbus and
the New World

Edited by
Joseph C. Schnaubelt, O.S.A.
and Frederick Van Fleteren

Prepared in Cooperation with
the Augustinian Historical Institute of Villanova University

PETER LANG
New York • Washington, D.C./Baltimore • Boston
Bern • Frankfurt am Main • Berlin • Vienna • Paris

Library of Congress Cataloging-in-Publication Data

Columbus and the New World / Joseph C. Schnaubelt and
Frederick Van Fleteren, editors.
p. cm. — (American university studies. IX: History; vol. 185)
Includes bibliographical references and index.
1. Columbus, Christopher—Congresses. 2. America—Discovery and
exploration—Spanish—Congresses. 3. Columbus, Christopher—Knowledge
and learning—Congresses. I. Van Fleteren, Frederick. II. Title. III. Series:
American university studies. Series IX: History, vol. 185.
ISBN 0-8204-3736-0
ISSN 0740-0462

Die Deutsche Bibliothek-CIP-Einheitsaufnahme

Columbus and the New World / Joseph C. Schnaubelt and
Frederick Van Fleteren, eds. –New York; Washington, D.C./Baltimore; Boston;
Bern; Frankfurt am Main; Berlin; Vienna; Paris: Lang.
(American university studies: 9: History; Vol. 185)
ISBN 0-8204-3736-0 Gb.

Prepared in Cooperation with
The Augustinian Historical Institute of Villanova University.

The paper in this book meets the guidelines for permanence and durability
of the Committee on Production Guidelines for Book Longevity
of the Council of Library Resources.

Printed in the United States of America.

Contents

vi *Contents*

Aftermath of the Voyage

Preface

In popular parlance, 1492 is called the year that "Columbus discovered America." The designation is inaccurate, for "America" had not yet been named and identified as a continent and (from the European perspective) a "New World." Columbus died thinking he had found a western route to *Cipangu*. Or was it *Cathay*? Or perhaps *India* or the *Indies*? Hart Crane, in his epic poem *The Bridge*, has Columbus wondering at the end of his voyage what he had actually found.

1492 is a date that changed the world (for both good and evil) as no other. 1066 changed England, 1776 changed the colonies, 1914 and 1939, the dates of World Wars I and II, changed the direction of the twentieth century; but 1492 divided world history into what it is today. It has no parallel in the past one thousand years.

As the quincentenary of Columbus's voyage of discovery in 1492 approached, the directors of the International Patristic, Mediaeval, and Renaissance Conference at Villanova University considered commemorating this momentous event. The interdisciplinary and cross-cultural character of the conference offered numerous options. The conference directors settled upon a three-year program examining (a) the "pulse" of the world on the eve of the discovery (1991 Conference), (b) the immediate events of 1492 (1992 Conference), and (c) the aftermath of the discovery (1993 Conference). A variety of topics was scheduled, and a volume projected.

The lectures of six plenary speakers and a select number of the shorter communications comprise the present volume. These articles and essays have been arranged under the following section headings: Prologue, Prolegomena to the Voyage, The Voyage, Aftermath of the Voyage. From the character and theme of the respective divisions, the significance of the "voyage of discovery" is set in proper historical perspective.

Section I ("Prologue") consists of three studies concerning the European intellectual milieu when Columbus was preparing his venture. The quincentenary has occasioned debate about Columbus's own motives and European goals, colonialism, racism, and religious persecution. Even greater controversy claims that Icelanders, specifically Lief Ericson, were the first European contact with the New World.

Kay Brigham analyzes Columbus's unpublished *Libro de las pro-*

fecías, a prime source for understanding Columbus's motivation in undertaking his unique voyage. In particular, the *Libro* discloses the breadth of Columbus's reading and his high esteem for Scripture; nothing is more germane to the issue of motivation than such original inspirations and statements. Subsequent essays refer to commercialism, competition among emerging political states, developing international law, and jurisdictional claims over newly discovered lands as added stimulating factors.

Vernon Bourke's study of Augustine's impact upon Columbus's ventures illustrates the unexpected depth of Columbus's readings. Currents of thought from ancient Greece and Rome, as well as early Christianity, were known and cited in Western European circles. Augustine did not support exploration of the "other side" of the world enthusiastically, but he did not assert with certitude that the earth was "flat."

Allan Bäck's study, the last in this Prologue-section, describes Arabic influence on the Christian West — specifically on science and philosophy — before, during, and after Columbus's voyages. Contrary to common opinion, Avicenna was an innovative voice in Arabic philosophy, his writings accelerating development of logic, categorization of sciences, improvement of medical practice, and design of astronomical instruments up to and beyond the "Discovery."

Section II ("Prolegomena") treats scientific events immediately germane to Columbus's voyages. George Saliba rectifies misapprehensions concerning Arabic astronomy during the "Age of Discovery." Arabic science was not in decline. On the contrary, Arabs were working diligently in astronomical theory, modifying such instruments as the astrolabe. These developments eventually reached the Latin West. Improvements in stellar navigation allowed sailors to plot courses with greater accuracy. To navigate, however, some grasp is necessary of where one is headed, where one is, and where one has been — thus the importance of mapping as preparation for Columbus's voyage. David Buisseret sketches the history of the development of maps and charts, from classical times to Columbus. At least in early times, maps were not merely geographical sketchings; rather they were similar to survey lists. Whether sailors' charts carrying indications of reefs, depths, wrecks or features of coastlines and waters, or religious pictures of the world, containing spiritual perspectives, which imposed biblical sites, descriptions and accounts upon the regions of the world depicted, mapmaking was an evolving and improving occupation. Growing commercialism awakened Columbus to the significance of maps. Such aids were critical for traders in order to save time and insure safety. Columbus himself engaged in mapping and charting, and appreciated the necessity of cartographic information for success in his venture.

Section III ("The Voyage") deals with numerous advances in navigation and naval architecture. Delno West discusses the all-important route and time line Columbus had to calculate in assessing the feasibility of his venture. His political support and financial backing, moreover, would depend upon this projection of success. He would also have to convince crewmen and navigators to commit themselves to the unknown peril of the "Ocean Sea." Many a listener to his plans considered Columbus a "dreamer."

Analyzing the naval science, vessels, and practices of fifteenth-century mariners, James E. Kelley, Jr. assesses Columbus's factual and theoretical achievements. Granted the significant advances in nearly all aspects of sea-faring prior to 1492 and Columbus's ability as a navigator, his achievement was still notable. Given the size of his ships, the length of his voyage, and the force of the Atlantic Ocean (especially at the time of year he set sail), it was a truly courageous enterprise.

Section IV ("Aftermath") consists of two reflections on cross-cultural influences. James Muldoon argues that the "New World" is to be understood in terms of the "Old," specifically in regard to civil politics and the relationship between church and state. European thinking about the "New World" remained moored in traditional thought patterns to which they forcibly accommodated the newly discovered lands and peoples. In short, how *new* the "New World" was would take centuries for Europeans to assimilate and appreciate.

In his essay, William H. McNeill avers that, because of biological interaction between various life forms, neither the "New World" nor the "Old" could remain unaffected. Only recently have historians addressed the migration of life forms between the two biospheres. McNeill alerts us to this novel approach to Columbus's voyage.

These studies furnish us a sense of this quincentennial celebration. Still they fall short of the "full picture." Vikings may have sailed to the "New World" before Columbus, but knowledge of their arrival comes primarily through Icelandic sagas and archaeological remains. By contrast, Columbus's discovery was a "media event."

In the latter half of the fourteenth century, bubonic plague claimed one-third of the population of Europe. Consequently, the ranks of European scholars, explorers, and inventors were decimated. Recovering slowly, by the fifteenth century the European community had gained a scientific and geographical knowledge which an emerging group of capitalists sought to exploit. Nevertheless, an enduring scarcity of men of ability may partially explain why the significance of Columbus's discovery was only gradually appreciated throughout Europe and Arabia. Indeed, even today, in many quarters, Columbus's voyage remains *terra incognita*.

On 4 October 1957, the first in a series of artificial earth satellites was launched by the U.S.S.R. It was called "Sputnik I," and with it the

"Space Age" was launched. What scientific accomplishments, political interests, inventor groups, capital and funds made this possible? The dawn of the space age in the twentieth century is strikingly similar to the voyage of Columbus. Our age is in addition the "information age." If the Admiral's accomplishment is indicative, it may take another five hundred years to sort out the full story of the beginning of space exploration.

Finally, we thank all who planned, coordinated, or participated in the three conferences at which these papers were delivered. It is only through such efforts that the Patristic, Mediaeval, and Renaissance Conference at Villanova University continues to flourish.

T.A. Losoncy
Augustinian Historical Institute
Villanova University

February 1996

I
Prologue

The Importance of the Book of Prophecies

in Understanding Columbus

Kay Brigham

"As a Man Thinketh, So Is He"

How can we know the heart and mind of a man who has been dead
for almost five hundred years? Proverbs 23:7 says: "As a man thinketh
in his heart, so is he." [1] We can apply that wisdom to understanding
Christopher Columbus, a man who has become a controversial figure on
the eve of the Quincentenary of his first voyage to the "Other World."
Admittedly Columbus is a complex personality, as are all human beings.
In his writings Columbus himself acknowledged his shortcomings and
expressed his trust in God:

> I am the worst of sinners. The pity and mercy of our Lord have com-
> pletely covered me whenever I have called [on him] for them. I have
> found the sweetest consolation in casting away all my anxiety, so as to
> contemplate his marvelous presence. (*Book of Prophecies*, folio 5 rvs.)

Yet the questions raised today about his character and motives do
not always stem from a concern for the whole truth and a genuine
desire to know the man and his times. For example, many revisionists
today have chosen to ignore the historical record of the Discovery or
distort it in order to promote their particular social and political agen-
das. In both the Old and New Worlds, Columbus-bashing has become
fashionable. The controversy underlines the importance of and need
for sound scholarship in appraising Columbus and the Great Encounter.

"A Most Rare Book"

Scholars have wondered and debated for centuries about what
truly motivated Christopher Columbus to voyage across an unknown
ocean to find the Indies. The best sources for getting at the truth are
the primary documents. If only Columbus could tell us himself, there

might be an end to the speculation and controversy which has intensified to this day.

All the while there was a manuscript writing by Columbus setting forth the Scriptures which motivated his voyages. It came to be known as *Libro de las profecías*. This writing of Columbus has escaped the attention of scholars for centuries. It lay in the venerable Biblioteca Colombina of the Cathedral of Seville where the moths and the rats studied and digested it more than any scholar read and analyzed its Latin and fifteenth century Spanish text. Only recently have a few scholars found and understood the *Book of Prophecies* and ended the obscurity which had hidden this valuable insight into the heart and mind of Columbus. The *Book of Prophecies* is an extraordinary, captivating writing, indeed a *raríssimo códice*—"a most rare book"—as one of the cathedral librarians commented many years ago.

The original manuscript of the *Book of Prophecies*, bound in vellum, consists of eighty-four numbered leaves (fourteen are missing), with writing on both the front and reverse sides. The complete title in Latin on the reverse side of folio 1 reads: "Book [of] authoritative quotations, sayings, pronouncements, and prophecies concerning the recuperation of the Holy City and the Mount of God, Zion, and concerning the finding and conversion of the islands of India and of all people and nations, to our Hispanic Sovereigns."

Columbus composed the *Book of Prophecies* in 1501-1502, after his third voyage. Because of his failure as an administrator on Hispaniola, he had been sent back to Spain in chains. While awaiting an audience with the Catholic sovereigns, the Admiral spent a period of time in the monastery of Santa María de las Cuevas in Seville. He had access to the monastery library and the help of his good friend, Gaspar Gorricio, a Carthusian monk. The *Book of Prophecies* is, for the most part, a collection of Columbus's personal studies. Four different handwritings, including Columbus's own calligraphy, painstakingly recorded hundreds of passages from the Bible and from the writings of the church fathers and other respected theologians (St. Augustine, Nicholas of Lyra, Pierre d'Ailly, and others), which the Admiral related to his enterprise of the Indies and to the recovery of the Holy City of Jerusalem. Columbus's aim was to explain to the Spanish sovereigns his vision and the significance of his discovery, in the light of authoritative writings and biblical prophecies.

The *Book of Prophecies* is in itself a wonderful discovery because it reconstructs the great navigator's image of himself as a man of destiny. He had an amazing awareness of his role in the scheme of world history. He believed the Lord had bestowed the gift of spiritual intelligence to equip him for his providential mission as "Christ-bearer." In Columbus's mind the evangelization of the newly discovered lands was to inaugurate the Messiah's kingdom in fulfillment of Isaiah's prophecy.

In the prefatory letter of the *Book of Prophecies* addressed to King Ferdinand and Queen Isabella, Columbus sets forth his vision of world history with these words:

> At this time I have seen and put in study to look into all the Scriptures . . . which our Lord opened to my understanding (I could sense his hand upon me), so that it became clear to me that it was feasible to navigate from here to the Indies; and he gave me the will to execute the idea. . . . I have already said that for the execution of the enterprise of the Indies, neither reason nor mathematics, nor world maps were profitable to me; rather the prophecy of Isaiah was completely fulfilled. And this is what I wish to report here for the consideration of your Highnesses, and because you will be gladdened by what I will tell you concerning Jerusalem by the same authoritative references. (*Book of Prophecies*, folios 4, 5 rvs.)

Christopher Columbus: Deliverer of Jerusalem

Christopher Columbus was well versed in the Old and New Testaments and the Apocrypha in the Vulgate Bible. Regarding hermeneutics, he quoted the scholastic writings, such as the *Summa* of Thomas Aquinas, and therefore was aware of the fourfold sense of Scripture. [2] He was especially fond of typology and the whole concept of promise-fulfillment. For example, David as the conqueror of Jerusalem from the Jebusites, was a type or model which inspired Columbus's role in history as the deliverer of the Holy City from the infidels.

The majority of the numerous biblical prophecies which Columbus cites in his compilation in the *Book of Prophecies* relate to the restoration and the future glory of Jerusalem. In the time of Columbus, the Holy Land was under Muslim control. The city of Constantinople, gateway to the Orient, fell into the hands of the Ottoman Turks in 1453. The encroachment of Islam provoked Europeans to search for new routes to Asia and awakened longings for a new crusade to liberate the Holy City of Jerusalem from Muslim domination. Any project that might frustrate Muslim aggression would find fertile ground in Spain, a nation imbued with a sense of messianism, acquired during the course of eight centuries of the Reconquest. The Moors had invaded the Iberian peninsula in 711 A.D. and were a deeply rooted presence until their final defeat at Granada in January of 1492. The Christian sovereigns of Spain in the late fifteenth and sixteenth centuries poured heart and soul into a national policy to achieve a religious unity, first in the Iberian peninsula, then in Europe and America. Columbus's discovery of America was in itself a victory over Islam, for it more than doubled the area of Christianity.

The great Columbian Enterprise proposed to navigate from Spain to the exotic India, Cathay (China), and Cipangu (Japan) by crossing the Ocean on a western course. In his letters to their Majesties the Admiral expressed time and again his earnest desire to dedicate a percentage of the revenues from the Indies to finance a great crusade to rescue the Holy Places in Jerusalem. For that reason he was looking for the mines of Solomon and the "gold of Ophir" in the distant islands of the sea. In the light of the biblical prophecies which promise "the restitution of the Holy Temple to the Holy Church," [3] Columbus urged Isabella and Ferdinand to undertake the conquest of Jerusalem:

> If there is faith, you are bound to have victory from the enterprise. Your Highnesses, remember the Gospel texts and the many promises which our Savior made to us. . . . The mountains will obey anyone who has the faith the size of a kernel of Indian corn. All that is requested by anyone who has faith will be granted. Knock and it will be opened to you. No one should be afraid to take on any enterprise in the name of our Savior, if it is right and if the purpose is purely for his holy service. . . . Remember, your Highnesses, that you undertook, at little cost, the enterprise [conquest] of the kingdom of Granada. (*Book of Prophecies*, folio 5 rvs.)

Furthermore, Columbus quoted twice the medieval prophecy of Joachim of Fiore that "the man who was to rebuild the Temple on Mount Zion would come out of Spain." [4]

We cannot judge, from a modern perspective, Columbus's messianism as "bizarre." His ideas were a product of the messianic spirit of the crusades in the Middle Ages.

Christopher Columbus: "Christ-Bearer" to the Distant Lands

Columbus interpreted the Scriptures he extracted for his compilation of the *Book of Prophecies* in a direct and personal way. He regarded himself as a servant of God like David or John the Baptist. The servant of the Lord is "a man to fulfill [God's] purpose" (Is 46:11) —that is, a man divinely appointed for an exalted mission, a "holy enterprise" to implement God's plan of salvation in history. In the *Book of Prophecies* the Admiral quoted extensively from the "Songs of the Lord's Servant" found in Isaiah:

> Here is my servant, whom I uphold, my chosen one in whom I delight;
> I will put my Spirit on him. . . . In his law the islands will put their

hope. . . . I, the Lord, have called you in righteousness; I will take hold
of your hand. I will keep you and make you to be a covenant for the
people and a light for the Gentiles. . . . Is 42:1,4,6 (*Book of Prophecies*,
folios 30 rvs., 31)

The Admiral firmly believed that his name "Christopher" was
given him, not by accident, but by the will of God to designate his mission. Thus almost all of Columbus's writings, from 1493 until his death
in 1506, show the signature "*Xpo Ferens.*" *Christo Ferens* is the Greco-
Latin form of his name Christopher, the significance of which emphasizes his highest mission as the "Christ-bearer," the one who carries the
saving name of Jesus to the inhabitants of the lands beyond the seas.

Indeed the great theme of the *Book of Prophecies* is the calling and
conversion of all the nations to the Christian faith. Columbus scrutin-
ized the Bible and the scholastic writings for enlightenment. He quoted
extensively from St. Augustine who commented on biblical passages,
such as Zephaniah 2:11: [5]

The LORD will be awesome to them when he destroys all the gods of
the land. The nations on every shore will worship him, every one in
its own land.

Columbus also believed that the preaching of the gospel to all the
nations was to hasten the return of Jesus Christ and the end of the
world. He writes in his prefatory letter to the Sovereigns thus:

The Holy Scriptures testify in the Old Testament, by the mouth of the
prophets, and in the New [Testament], by our Savior Jesus Christ, that
this world will come to an end: Matthew, Mark, and Luke have
recorded the signs of the end of the age; the prophets had also abundantly foretold it. . . . And I say that the sign which convinces me that
our Lord is hastening the end of the world is the preaching of the
Gospel recently in so many lands. (*Book of Prophecies*, folios 5, 6)

Addressing the Sovereigns, Columbus expressed his keen sense of
mission and complete trust in God's sovereignty over history:

I found our Lord well-disposed toward my heart's desire, and he gave
me the spirit of intelligence for the task. . . . Who doubts that this
illumination was from the Holy Spirit? He [the Spirit], with marvelous rays of light, consoled me through the holy and sacred Scriptures,
a strong and clear testimony, . . . encouraging me to proceed, and,
continually, without ceasing for a moment, they inflame me with a
sense of great urgency. . . . The working out of all things was entrusted

by our Lord to each person, [but it happens] in conformity with his sovereign will, even though he gives advice to many. He lacks nothing that it may be in the power of men to give him. O, how good is the Lord who wishes people to perform that for which he holds himself responsible! Day and night, and at every moment, everyone should give him their most devoted thanks. (*Book of Prophecies*, folios 4, 5 rvs., 6)

Certain of his destined role in history to fulfill biblical prophecy on a global scale, Columbus quoted Psalm 19:4 five times throughout the *Book of Prophecies*:

Their voice goes out into all the earth, their words to the ends of the world.

And indeed the gospel was first preached in the New World in the Spanish language.

The Power of Faith

The "discovery" of Christopher Columbus's *Book of Prophecies* has brought to light the faith and vision of a mariner whose exploit broke the chains of the mighty Ocean Sea and opened up the "Other World," in fulfillment of Seneca's famous first-century prophecy in Medea:

An age will come after many years, when the Ocean will loose the chains of things, and a great land will lie revealed; and a mariner, like Tiphys who was Jason's guide, will discover a new world, and then the island of Thule [Iceland] will no longer be the ultimate. (*Book of Prophecies*, folio 59 rvs.)

The essence of Columbus—his genuine and constant spirituality— is evident throughout all his prolific writings from 1481, when he was about thirty years of age, to the end of his life in 1506. This spirituality appears strange to and baffles the modern mind, but its power and influence in the life and work of Columbus are undeniable. What is clear is the importance of the *Book of Prophecies* as a unique record of the medieval scholastic formation and deep biblical faith of a merchant-seaman who directed the course of history into the future.

Notes

[1] The first biblical quote is taken from the *King James Version*; the rest are from the *New International Version* (Grand Rapids: Zondervan, 1978).

[2] (1) the historical or literal sense; (2) the allegorical sense; (3) the tropological or moral sense; (4) the anagogical sense.

[3] *Book of Prophecies*, folio 4.

[4] *Book of Prophecies*, folios 6, 67 rvs.

[5] *The City of God*, Book 18, Chapter 33.

St. Christopher the Christ-bearer: detail from the map of Juan de la Cosa, 1500

Facsimile of *Libro de las profecías*: one of the most fascinating pages from the *Book of Prophecies* was written completely in Columbus's own hand. The verso folio bears Hispano-Roman philosopher Seneca's first-century prophecy from *Medea* and Columbus's own account of two eclipses of the moon he witnessed in the New World — one in Hispaniola and one in Jamaica. Photograph by Amy Brigham Boulris.

Augustine and Columbus' Voyages

Vernon J. Bourke

The five-hundredth anniversary of Christopher Columbus' discovery of the New World calls for some consideration of the influence of earlier Christian writers on the Commodore's decision to sail to the uncharted West. One of the key figures in this background was Augustine of Hippo. It is still sometimes said that, before Columbus, people thought that the earth was flat and, if one sailed to the edge of it, one would fall off. Doubtless this flat-earth view was common in the early centuries of the Christian era, even though a good many ancient philosophers and scientists thought the earth to be spherical.

However, in the first decade of the fourth century, the Christian rhetor, Caecilius Firmianus Lactantius, wrote that, "it is absurd (*ineptum*) to believe that there are men whose footsteps are higher than their heads, or that down there the things in our surroundings are suspended upside-down; that plants and trees grow downward, and so on." [1] Later in the same chapter of his *Institutiones diuinae*, Lactantius added that the origin of this error was in the philosophers who thought that the world is round (*rotundum esse mundum*). Four centuries later, Pope Zacharias wrote a letter to Boniface (A.D. 748) which condemned the "perverse and evil teaching of someone named Virgillius who claimed that another world and other men existed underneath the earth." [2]

Midway in time between these two spokesmen for Christian thinking is a much better educated Saint and Father of the Church, Augustine of Hippo. He represents what was thought by many in the fifth century. Augustine took a more broad-minded position on the shape of the earth. He did not reject the sphericity of the earth but rather had serious doubts that there were men on its other side. In any case he felt that it was hardly possible to sail down there over the vast Ocean (which he never saw) and find out the truth of the matter.

There is no doubt that Christopher Columbus knew about Augustine's views on this subject. In Fernando Columbo's biography of his father, we find the following: "in chapter 9 of Book XXI of the *De ciuitate dei*, the Saint denies the existence of the Antipodes and holds it impossible to pass from one hemisphere to the other." There follows a paragraph in which the son states various objections brought up in Spain to Christopher's plan to sail westward to India. And Fernando adds, "The Admiral gave suitable replies to all these objections." [3]

Actually the key passage in the *De ciuitate dei* is not in Book XXI, but it is clear that this text from Augustine was well known in fifteenth-century Spain. Immediately before the sentence quoted above, Fernando remarked that Christopher's opponents "all repeated the Spanish saying that is commonly used of any doubtful statement, 'St. Augustine doubts' . . ."

Augustine on the Shape of the Earth

Actually St. Augustine's influence on Christopher Columbus' plans was not entirely negative. Augustine never really denied that the earth is spherical. He did say, of course, that this was not something that the ordinary Christian had to be concerned about. Preaching on Psalm 95 (96), verse 13, which speaks of Yahweh coming to "judge the earth" (*judicare terram*), Augustine remarked that the Christian "pays no attention to the shape of the world (*mundus*)." "I wish you," he tells his congregation, "to be without concern for this." [4] Later in the same sermon we find Augustine using, not the term "world" (*mundus*) but the very common biblical phrase "*orbis terrarum*" (the orb of the earths). Commenting on this, Augustine says that God, "gathers together [for judgment] all the elect from the four winds: so, from the whole orb of the earths." [5] English versions usually ignore the word *orbis* here, as in the frequent occurrences in Scripture, and simply say, "the whole earth." In Latin, as still in English, an orb is a globe. In a secondary sense it is applied to a circular path followed by a star, that is, an orbit. [6]

Explaining another Psalm, [7] where it is written that, "his empire shall stretch from sea to sea, from the river to the ends of the earth" (*ad terminos orbis terrae*), Augustine says that the earth is something like an island surrounded by the Ocean, and that the Christian Church has reached some areas in the West but there are other parts that Christianity will reach in the future. [8] Clearly Augustine thinks that the land mass on earth extends farther westward than has yet been reached and that Christians will get there in times to come. In various places, Augustine points out that, when it is time for the world to end, "the Gospel will be proclaimed in the whole sphere (*in universo orbe*), as a witness to all peoples, and then the end will come" (Mt 24:14) [9]

What further confuses literal readers of such passages in the Old and New Testaments is the frequent reference to the "ends of the earth" (*ad terminos — uel fines — terrae*), or to the four winds (north, south, east, west) indicating terminal directions (*a quattuor uentis*). It was difficult for premodern people to avoid thinking that there is an absolute north and south, east and west, just as it was hard not to think that there is an absolute up and down. Strangely, Augustine noticed that the Greek names for the four winds (*Anatole, Dustis, Arkton* and *Mesembein*) began with letters that spelled

ADAM. This stimulated the conviction that all over the earth the descendants of the first man would eventually be discovered and taught the true religion. [10]

The Three Continents Known to Augustine

For Augustine, three continents made up the land mass on earth. They were Asia, Europe and Africa. An interesting passage in the *De ciuitate dei* shows this clearly:

> In fact [he writes], the well-known ruler Ninus, son of Belus, had subdued the whole of Asia except India, and by Asia I mean, not just what is now the Roman province of Asia, but the whole continent of Asia (*sed eam quae universa Asia nuncupatur*) which is sometimes reckoned as a half or, more commonly, as a third of the whole world, which consists of Asia, Europe and Africa. These three continents are not equal in size. Continental Asia stretches far to the south, to the east and to the north; Europe, to the north and west; Africa to the west and south. Thus, Europe and Africa take up one half of the world, and Asia the other. [11]

At various places in his works, Augustine names many different peoples that inhabit these continents. Besides the Greeks, there are wise men in Atlantic Lybia, Egypt, India, Persia, Chaldaea, Scythia, Gaul and Spain. [12] Earlier in the *De ciuitate dei*, [13] he speaks of the early Romans, the Assyrians, Persians and Hebrews. Of course the Jewish people are noted in many places [14] as witnesses to the Scripture and as consecrated to the city of God. This gives us some idea of the scope of Augustine's geographic and demographic knowledge. He was by no means limited to his own little region on the north of Africa.

People on the Other Side of the Earth

Augustine did face the problem of the possible existence of human beings on the other side of the terrestrial globe. The fact that he even mentions this possibility shows that he was convinced that there is another side. But he leaves no doubt as to his own view of such people. In *De ciuitate dei* XVI,9, which Columbus' son, Fernando, mentioned as *De ciuitate dei* XXI, Augustine said:

> As to the nonsense about there being antipodes, that is to say, men living on the far side of the earth, where the sun rises when it sets for us, men who have their feet facing ours when they walk — that is utterly incredible (*nulla ratione credendum est*). No one pretends

to have any factual information, but a hypothesis is reached by the argument that the earth is suspended between the celestial hemispheres and since the universe must have a similar lowest and central point, therefore the other portion of the earth which is below us cannot be without inhabitants.

One flaw in the argument is that, even if the universe could be proved by reasoning to be shaped like a round globe — or at least believed to be so — it does not follow that the other hemisphere of the earth must appear above the surface of the ocean, or if it does, there is no immediate necessity why it should be inhabited by men. First of all, our Scriptures never deceive us, since we can test the truth of what they have told us by the fulfillment of predictions; second, it is utterly absurd to say that any men from this side of the world could sail across the immense tract of the ocean and reach the far side (*nimisque absurdum est ut dicatur aliquos homines, ex hac in illam partem, Oceani immensitate trajecta, nauigare et peruenire potuisse*), and then people it with men sprung from the single father of all mankind. [15]

The Spanish opponents of Christopher Columbus' plan to sail directly to India, going westward, did find some support in the *De ciuitate dei*. Quite probably Augustine did think that the earth is a sphere, but he tended to discourage any attempt to sail to its other side. As he admitted at the end of the famous text just quoted:

Let us be content, then, to limit our search for the citizens of the pilgrim City of God on earth to those races of men which, as we have seen, were made up of the seventy-two nations, each with its own language. [16]

If Columbus had taken Augustine's advice seriously, the discovery of America might have been much delayed.

Notes

[1] Lactantius, *Institutiones diuinae* III,24: *PL* VI,425: *ineptum credere esse homines quorum uestigia sunt superiora quam capita, aut ibi quae apud nos jacent in uersa pendere; fruges et arbores deorsum uersus crescere* (Cited by the Benedictine Editors in the Maurist ed. of *De ciuitate dei* XVI,9, in the *Opera Omnia S. Augustini*, reprinted Venice, 1722 = *PL* XL,487, n. a.)

[2] Pope Zacharias (741-752), *Epistula X* ad Bonifacium, is also quoted by the Benedictines in the same place: *perversam et iniquam* [appellat] *doctrinam* [Virgilii cujusdam asserentis] *quod alius mundus et alii homines sub terra sint.*

[3] Fernando Colombo, *The Life of the Admiral Christopher Columbus by His Son Ferdinand*, trans. B. Keen (Westport, CT 1978; reprinted from the Rutgers University edition of 1959), 39. Earlier (page 17), Fernando cited as the bases of his father's response to such objections the views of Aristotle's *De caelo et mundo* with the commentaries thereon of Avorroës and Thomas Aquinas, plus Seneca's *Quaestiones Naturales*. As Fernando puts it, these scholars held that, "a ship could sail from the end of Spain to the Indies in a few days." (It may be noted that Aquinas' *Commentarium Aristotelis de caelo et mundo* II,i,27,n. 543, where Aristotle demonstrates that the earth is spherical, gives a remarkably accurate estimate of the number of miles per degree of longitude.)

[4] *Enarratio in Psalmum XCV* 14: *PL* XXXVII,1235: *Praeterit enim figura hujus mundi. Volo vos sine sollicitudine esse.*

[5] *Enarratio in Psalmum XCV* 15: *PL* XXXVII,1236: *Congregat omnes electos a quattuor ventis: ergo de toto orbe terrarum.*

[6] Thus *Dictionnaire Latin-Français*, compiled by A. Gariel (Paris 1915), 346: *orbis: cercle, globe, monde, cours (astre), orbite.* Similarly, *Webster's Collegiate Dictionary* (1948), 697: "orb: 1. A spherical body; esp. a celestial sphere; Obs. the earth."

[7] *Enarratio in Psalmum LXXI* 11: *PL* XXXVI,908.

[8] *Epistula CXCIX* XII,47: *PL* XXXIII,923: *tamquam omnium quodammodo maximo est insula, quia et ipsam cingit Oceanus, ad cujus littora in occidentalibus partibus Ecclesiam pervenisse jam novimus et quocumque littoram nondum pervenit, perventura est utique fructificando atque crescendo.*

[9] Matthew 24:14 is cited by Augustine in *Epistula XCIII*; *Epistula CXL*; *Epistula CLXXXVI*; *Epistula CLXXXVII*; *Epistula CXCVII*; *Enarratio in Psalmum LXXI* 11; *Enarratio in psalmum CI, Sermo II* 9 and 12; *Enarratio in psalmum CXXXIV*. The Vulgate version reads: *praedicabitur hoc Evangelium in universo orbe in testimonium omnibus gentibus, et tunc veniet finis.*

[10] *In Ioannis Euangelium tractatus* IX,14: *CC* XXXVI,98; a similar speculation about the winds and the acronym, ADAM, is found in *Enarratio in Psalmum XCV* 15: *PL* XXXVII,1236.

[11] *De ciuitate dei* XVI,17: *CSEL* XL(2),159: *Nam rex ille Ninus Beli filius, excepta India, universae Asiae populos subiugauerat. Asiam nunc dico, non illam partem quae huius maioris Asiae una prouincia est, sed eam quae uniuersa Asia nuncupatur, quam quidam in altera duarum, plerique autem in tertia totius orbis parte posuerunt, ut sint omnes, Asia, Europa, et Africa: quod non aequali diuisione fecerunt. Namque ista quae Asia nuncupatur, a meridie per orientem usque ad septentrionem peruenit: Europa uero a septentrione usque ad occidentem; atque inde Afria ab occidente usque ad meridiem. Unde uidentur orbem dimidium duae tenere, Europa et Africa, alium uero dimidium sola Asia.* Translation of *City of God* is by G.G. Walsh et al. (Garden City, NY 1958), 371.

[12] *De ciuitate dei* VIII,9: *CC* XLVII,225-26.

[13] *De ciuitate dei* V,21: *CC* XLVII,157-58.

[14] See, for example, *De ciuitate dei* VII,32: *CC* XLVII,213; X,32: *CC* XLVII, 311.

[15] *De ciuitate dei* XVI,9: *CSEL* XL(2),142: *Quod uero et Antipodas esse fabulantur, id est, homines a contraria parte terrae, ubi sol oritur, quando occidit nobis, aduersa pedibus nostris calcare uestigia, nulla ratione credendum est. Neque hoc ulla historica cognitione didicisse se affirmant, sed quasi ratiocinando coniectant, eo quod intra conuexa caeli terra supensa sit, eumdemque locum mundus habeat, et infimum, et medium: et ex hoc opinantur alteram terrae partem, quae infra est, habitatione hominum carere non posse. Nec attendunt, etiamsi figura conglobata et rotunda mundus esse credatur, siue aliqua ratione monstretur; non tamen esse consequens, ut etiam ex illa parte ab aquarum congerie nuda sit terra: deinde etiamsi nuda sit, neque hoc statim necesse esse, ut homines habeat. Quoniam nullo modo Scriptura ista mentitur, quae narratis praeteritis facit fidem, eo quod eius praedicta complentur: nimisque absurdum est, ut dicatur aliquos homines ex hac in illam partem, Oceani immensitate traiecta, nauigare ac peruenire potuisse, ut etiam illic ex uno illo primo homine genus institueretur humanum (City of God* [Image Book], 367-68).

[16] Ibid.: *Quapropter inter illos tunc hominum populos, qui per septuaginta duas gentes et totidem linguas colliguntur fuisse diuisa, quaeramus si possumus inuenire illam in terris peregrinantem ciuitatem Dei* . . .

Avicenna in the Age of Columbus

Allan Bäck

Husein Ibn Sina (Avicenna) was a Persian Muslim philosopher who flourished in the eleventh century a.d. His work greatly influenced such medieval philosophers as Albert the Great, Thomas Aquinas, Roger Bacon, Raymond Lull, Duns Scotus, and William Ockham. Less obvious is what influence he had upon Western Philosophy in the Renaissance and beyond. It is clear that his works were widely available: the great printed editions of the *Avicenna Latinus* appeared at the start of the sixteenth century. These editions would have been read and used at least by the second scholastics. But did Avicenna contribute to the development of modern philosophy, so often symbolized by the passage of Columbus to the New World?

During the early modern period, scholastics studied and discussed works of Avicenna, at least those available in Latin translation, both via secondary sources and in the primary texts themselves,. Avicenna also influenced non-scholastic, "modern philosophers" such as Descartes and Kant. The congruence of doctrine is so strong as to warrant suspicion of some direct influence by Avicenna.

Treatment of corporeal substance is an example of such influence. For Avicenna the issue of how quiddities in themselves come to be *in re* and become capable of assuming accidental material and spatial attributes is central. Likewise, in modern times, this issue — the nature of the things studied by physics — is crucial.

Summary of Avicenna's Views [1]

For Avicenna quiddities or essences exist in three respects: in themselves, with respect to what is stated in their definitions; in individuals, insofar as they exist *in re* as constituting material objects; and in the mind, insofar as they are known and exist *in intellectu*. Here we are concerned mostly with the passage from quiddities in themselves to quiddities in individuals.

Most quiddities in themselves, except for the most general, have essential components, as revealed in their definitions. Thus, as "man" is "rational animal," the quiddity in itself, humanity, consists of animality and rationality; likewise animality consists of animation and motion and organism. Attributes that are necessarily concomitant with the essential attributes (namely, *propria*) are not essential components of a quiddity in itself. So risibility is not an essential component of humanity. Some quiddities in themselves are such that their definitions do not require nor rule out their existence *in re*. Hence they are possible beings. Now, there must be a sufficient reason determining whether they exist or do not exist. Since things do exist and possible beings cannot provide by themselves a sufficient ground for actual existence, Avicenna claims, there must be a quiddity, a unique one, that has existence necessarily, the necessary being or God. The necessary being is the cause of the existence of possible beings, the other quiddities in themselves, coming to exist *in re*.

Avicenna sees a certain necessary progression in how quiddities in themselves can come to exist *in re*. First, a quiddity in itself in the category of substance, on the most specific level (namely, an *infima species*), is put into a state able to have quiddities other than its essential components attached to it. This receptive state is called the matter. Then the quiddity in itself, corporeity, or being a body, must be attached to the substantial quiddity. Then follow the other accidents: first the ones following necessarily from the definition of the substantial quiddity in itself (namely, the *propria*), and, next, the purely accidental ones that come and go, like shape, measure, color, disposition, and relation.

For example, Socrates is produced (in the logical, not in the natural order) thus: The quiddity in itself, humanity, is put by an external cause into matter, that is, into a condition able to receive other quiddities in themselves that are not in the definition of humanity. Humanity is then connected to corporeity, and so becomes something occupying space. Now a corporeal thing existing *in re*, it may receive other, accidental quiddities in themselves: a humanoid shape, a color, various intellectual and moral traits, and can persist through time while changing those accidental traits, until the substantial substratum dissolves upon the approach of hemlock. Such is the history of Socrates.

By corporeity, Avicenna means extension, the ability to occupy space, in the sense of a featureless continuum wherein material objects may move and exist *in re*. For Avicenna, it is not part of the definition of corporeity to be three-dimensional. Rather, corporeity is a spatial continuum with an indeterminate numbers of dimensions. After the attachment of corporeity, of an indeterminate number of dimensions, to a substantial quiddity in itself, like humanity, the dimensions become determinate in number. Avicenna says that we "postulate" that there are three dimensions through a thought experiment. First we think of a line, and put another perpendicular to it, and then a third line perpendicular to both. As we find that we cannot go on, we postulate only three dimensions. (Note that current thought experiments are more complex, and we postulate more dimensions!)

Once the humanity has become three-dimensional, the quiddity divisibility may be attached. If so, the substance becomes terrestial and perishable; if not, celestial and imperishable. All these attributes will be essential constituents or *propria* of the individual substance. Next, it can receive a definite shape and other, contingent and changeable accidental attributes. For now a material substratum has been completed. [2] For Avicenna then, corporeity, that is, being extended, is not essential to the substantial quiddity in itself but only to its material existence. Corporeity is a *proprium*, a necessary accident of material existence, but not a genus, of the individual sensible substance. [3]

Avicenna and the Second Scholastics

Of course, Avicenna had great influence on Latin medieval philosophy, as can easily be established by the explicit citations of his work made by such major philosophers as Aquinas, Scotus, and Ockham. In later centuries he had at least an indirect influence, as his views were often cited in discussions of earlier medieval philosophers by the post-medieval (second) scholastics.

In the fifteenth century Plato and an Aristotle purified from scholastic barbarisms were in vogue. Yet at the same time Averroism was flourishing in Italy, especially in Padua. [4] Interest in Islamic culture was growing in this century; scholars going to Byzantium for the original texts of Plato and Aristotle also returned with manuscripts of Avicenna and Averroës. The fall of Constantinople, in 1453, gave Europe more direct contact with Muslims.

So there was renewed interest in things Islamic in the fifteenth century, especially in Italian universities like Naples and Padua. Despite the ascendancy of Averroës, Avicenna was not neglected. New translations of Avicenna's works, especially those relevant to medicine, were made by Andreas Alpagus and others. [5] As Averroës (Ibn Rushd) often stated his views in opposition to Avicenna's, Averroists read works of both philosophers. [6] This trend continued in the sixteenth century. For instance, Franciscus Toletus, Galileo's teacher at Padua, sided with Averroës against Avicenna, and held that there may be demonstrations of the fact (*quia*; *hoti*) as well as those of the reasoned fact (*propter quid*; *dihoti*). [7]

Again, scholastics would read Avicenna with reference to his being cited by Aquinas, Scotus, and Ockham. For example, Cajetan (Thomas de Vio), in his commentary on Aquinas' *De ente et essentia*, given at Padua in 1493-1494, quotes Avicenna extensively. [8] Domingo de Soto cited. and read Avicenna on the nature of falling bodies; Soto's works were later used by Galileo. [9] Later, in the sixteenth centure, Suarez will cite Avicenna regularly as one of the philosophers with whom he must deal as *auctoritates*. [10]

So then Avicenna's works continued to be used and cited by the second scholastics, those philosophers who continued and modified the traditions of the medieval schools in the modern period. The citations, at least by the more conscientious authors, were made by studying Avicenna's works directly, and not by merely copying earlier references to them. His works had, after all, become more widely available. For the Venice editions of the *Avicenna Latinus* at the beginning of the sixteenth century indicate a continuing interest in studying his work directly in the Renaissance. And, of course, with these printed editions, his work became more widely available.

Avicenna in the Renaissance

Though Muslim, Avicenna, along with Averroës, had great standing among Christians in the Renaissance. To be sure, they end up in Dante's Hell, but in Limbo with the philosophers like Plato and Aristotle, and not further down with Muhammid and Ali. [11] Evidently their philosophical labors generated enough Christian merit to move them up. Indeed, Dante uses Avicenna's theory of the celestial spheres and their emanation from God as the blueprint for constructing his picture of Paradise. [12] Dante had detailed knowledge of Islamic culture, and may have modeled the plot of his *Divine Comedy* on the Muslim legend of the nocturnal journey and ascension of Muhammid. [13]

Avicenna had a particularly high status in Italy on account of his work in medicine, notably the *Canon*, given the Italian preeminence in things medical. As I have noted, new translations were made of his works, especially those relevant to medicine. [14] Indeed, the content of the *Avicennae Opera* published at Venice twice, in 1495 and 1508, stresses natural science. His medical works continued to be used in European universities until the nineteenth century.

Italians instrumental in beginning the scientific revolution had some interest in Avicenna. Galileo had read Avicenna's logic and participated with Toletus in the disputes like the one about demonstrations of the fact mentioned above. Moreover he doubtless knew Avicenna's work on physics, especially his views on space. For in the fifteenth century, perhaps in revolt against medieval scholastic Aristotelianism, the view of space as a container-contained relation of place was attacked and supplanted by a view of space as an infinite receptacle with dimensions. Few medievals had held this view, and those few were nominalists, like Buridan and Albert of Saxony. Nominalism still dominated in the fifteenth century, although occasionally it was rejected vigorously. [15]

Buridan had his commentary on the *Physics* published in 1509 at Paris with a contemporary commentary by Dullaert; likewise for Albert of Saxony, published 1518 at Paris with George Lokert's commentary. [16] Here humanist interests contributed to this trend: a direct translation of John Philoponus's commentary on the *Physics* where the dimensional view of space is championed appears and was studied in the sixteenth century. As Avicenna holds and advocates the dimensional view, his works were studied too. In 1580 at Venice Toletus published his commentary on the *Physics* in line with this tradition. [17] Indeed, he championed Avicenna's views on space, as developed by the Mertonian calculators, Domingo de Soto, and Giovan Benedetti, against the Averroists. [18]

His student, Galileo, was familiar with all this. While at the University of Pisa, Galileo cited Philoponus and Avicenna repeatedly in his notebooks. He also cited even more frequently philosophers like Averroës, Albert the Great, Aquinas, and various Thomists, all of whom follow Avicenna's doctrines to some extent. [19] Most of his citations concern doctrines about the physical nature of matter: condensation, rarification, projectile motion on the Earth and in the heavens.

Likewise, Giordano Bruno had a conception of universal matter as pure extension without particular shape or dimensions. [20] In Avicenna, as I have noted, matter, the ability of quiddities in themselves in different categories to combine, is separate from extension, which again is separate from space, that is, three-dimensional extension. Yet in the early modern period matter, extension, and space all tend to be amalgated, as we shall see again with Descartes. Bruno too was following the dimensional view of space, although there is not enough detail to warrant a claim of his direct dependence on medieval sources. However, Bruno does cite Averroës occasionally in *De la causa*. [21]

So then Avicenna had considerable influence in the Renaissance, particularly on the notion of space, and thus had importance for modern physics. Surely, the primacy of corporeity is a plausible ancestor for Galileo's insistence on the ultimate reality of primary qualities in physics, as well as for Newtonian absolute space.

Again, the nature of space has some relevance to developing theories of projectile motion: it is one thing for an arrow in flight to be analyzed in terms of a passage from container to container, and another in terms of a passage through a three-dimensional receptacle without local features: on the former model, the Aristotelians had to explain the passage of the arrow as being occasioned by the local air of its container pushing it along; on the latter, the moderns could appeal to an impetus which would produce motion without end in an empty space and which would cease producing motion only when another force counteracted it.

Indeed, the impetus theory also traces its roots to Philoponus and Avicenna: "Avicenna is certainly one of the key links in the development and transmission of the impetus theory." [22] It was Avicenna's version of the impetus theory that influenced the medieval West the most, especially through Al-Ghazali's summary of it. [23] For Avicenna a motion communicated to a celestial substance would give it a perpetual impetus whose motive power would be conserved until some cause external to it negated that power. [24] This theory was then endorsed by nominalists like Buridan, Albert of Saxony, and Domingo de Soto. [25] Galileo, as well as Leonardo da Vinci, read and followed these views. [26] Indeed, it was Soto who formulated the law attributed to Galileo that the speed of a falling body is proportional to the time elapsed. [27]

Thus these modern views on projectile motion can be traced back to a theory held by Philoponus and Avicenna who held, against Aristotle and Averroës, that for celestial substances at least there need not be an external mover always pushing, in contact with the projectile for it to move. Now they did hold that terrestial substances, as they have a substantial nature that resists certain changes in place, do require a mover and do not conserve motion. The innovation of Galileo and his successors, like Descartes, was to extend the celestial account to the terrestial world. For Galileo denied the distinction of terrestial and celestial mechanics. So too Descartes extends "to all the parts of a uniform space the divine conservation of motion formerly restricted to the heavenly bodies." [28]

We may conclude then that the works of Avicenna were known and used by figures active in the Renaissance: poets, medical doctors, physicists.

Avicenna and Modern Philosophers

Less known and less obvious is the influence that Avicenna has had on modern philosophers. As with many scholastic doctrines that appear in modern philosophy, there arises the problem of transmission of doctrines of Avicenna to thinkers in a century as late as the seventeenth. Most prominent is the issue of over-determination. Doctrines of Avicenna could be learned directly, from the *Avicenna Latinus*, indirectly, through the primary sources of Averroës and Latin medieval philosophers, secondary sources on them, or contemporary scholastic textbooks, and even recreated *de novo*, through the individual genius of a great philosopher. Descartes started the fashion of pretending to begin *de novo*. So we do not have much testimony from them about their sources; likewise we should not construe their not citing Avicenna explicitly as decisive evidence that they did not use his work. Moreover, current scholarship in modern philosophy has not concentrated on ascertaining their sources. Some striking similarities between modern philosophy and Avicenna exist.

Descartes

Of course, as Descartes did research in physiology and physics, what I have said about Avicenna's thought on these topics in the Renaissance will apply to Descartes as well. Being in the tradition of the Renaissance humanists, Descartes too would have had occasion to consult the three-dimensional theory of space and the medical treatises of Avicenna. [29]

Now Descartes sometimes voices anti-scholastic sentiments. He was educated at the College of La Flèche in the Spanish Jesuit tradition. [30] He then speaks of the "errors of my youth" (for example, in *Meditation 1*), referring to his scholastic training. [31] Still Descartes may have rejected some scholastic doctrines without rejecting them all. Surely this is evident, given his use of an a posteriori argument for the existence of God in *Meditation 3*, and the ontological one in *Meditation 5*. He did study Augustine and Aquinas extensively; via Aquinas he would have had at least an indirect acquaintance with Avicenna 's work. [32] In any case, as I shall now show, Descartes and Avicenna have striking similarities of doctrine.

According to some scholars Descartes had two theories of space, one early and one mature. On both views it is essential to a body to be extended. On his early view, the extension of a body consists not merely in its occupying space, but in its occupying space with particular magnitudes of length, width, and depth. On this view, a body never changes its extension, that is, its shape. Still, a body, like a piece of wax, seems to change its shape. However Descartes has an atomist view, according to which the extension of a body is the sum of the extension of its constituent particles. [33] So the specific extension of each particle is fixed and immutable; changes in the shape of the whole stem from changes in the arrangement of its particles. (This early view seems to resemble the Aristotelian place, in that the particle might be said to carry its container about with it.)

Descartes may have considered his early view one of the errors of his youth. At any rate, he seems to have changed his mind. On his later view, the extension essential to body consists in being extended in space, in being a three-dimensional object. [34] The particular magnitudes of a body's shape do not constitute its extension. Rather, matter *qua* extended substance constitutes space. [35] Matter is a single continuous infinite whole, wherein local motions of particles may occur in vortices. A vortex of particles constitutes an individual body with its particular dimensions. So then, on his mature view, Descartes holds that to be a body is to occupy space, and to take on attributes of magnitude and dimension. This view strongly resembles Avicenna's conception of corporeity. [36]

Indeed, the famous wax example of *Meditation 2* strongly suggests that Descartes is using Avicenna's views explicitly. [37] Avicenna himself uses wax to illustrate his claim that the actual, measured dimensions of an individual substance are quantitative accidents, and are not essential to the substance. For they change while the substance remains. Rather, he says, only corporeity, in the sense of an indefinite multi-dimensional continuum, belongs to the materially existent substance:

> And if you take a candle [Latin: *ceram*] and then shape it in a shape for which dimensions in act are determined between those limits as numbered, definite, and measured, then, when you change that shape, nothing of the dimensions will remain in act as one for the individual through that definition and through that measure. Rather you will find other dimensions different from those in number. These dimensions belong to the class of quantity. [38]
>
> And the first body may exist insofar as it happens to it that it differs in virtue of quantity while it does not differ in virtue of the form. So there is preservation of the candle, whatever shape it has, such that it be, insofar as a determination of three simple dimensions is set in it in accordance with the form mentioned. And that does not differ in it [the candle], whereas there is a difference in it with every shape that is definite and specified in it [and that has] dimensions, in height and in width and in depth, in act or in potency, when that shape is definite. So if the wax is shaped by the shape of a sphere, then it is an occasion for the attribution of definite dimensions that are other than the definite, specified ones, which it received when its shape is a cubical shape, and that is its quantity. Therefore its substance may be preserved as a liquid, and may increase in volume in rarification. [39]

Likewise, Descartes, after dismissing the non-quantitative accidents of a piece of wax as irrelevant to its continued existence, proceeds to consider it as "something extended, flexible, and changeable." [40] He then relegates flexibility and mutability to secondary status, just as Avicenna did with divisibility — for the same reason: the extension can be conceived clearly and distinctly independently of those accidents. Descartes points out too that even the extension, namely, the actual dimensions of the wax, changes so much that we cannot imagine it clearly — for example, when the wax is heated and rarified. So he likewise rejects the quantitative properties as essential to the wax. Descartes says that still we know the individual piece of wax, "this particular piece of wax." But we do not know it through the senses or imagination. Rather our knowledge of the individual thing is given in a perception that is "a case of . . . pure mental scrutiny, and this can be imperfect and confused as it was before, or clear and distinct as it is not." [41] The intuitive perception is of the thing as extended in three dimensions. [42] Likewise, Avicenna says that we know an individual substance as such through direct intuition. Moreover, just as Descartes gives primacy to the material individual as an extended thing, so too Avicenna gives precedence to its corporeity, the thing in space. The main difference here is that Descartes appears more ready to commit himself to a three-dimensional space; Ibn Sina at first requires only an n-dimensional space, which he later concludes by thought experiment to have n = 3. [43] Indeed Avicenna and Descartes share so many views on this topic that Avicenna might as well have written Descartes' reply to Gassendi: "I did not abstract the concept of the wax from the concept of its accidents. Rather, I wanted to show how the substance of the wax is revealed by means of its accidents." [44]

So Descartes' use of the wax example has a striking resemblance in detail to Avicenna's views. Moreover, we have seen that the Cartesian theory (theories) of space, whatever the details turn out to be, falls into the tradition of Avicenna's view of corporeity. [45]

Finally, it is worth noting the similarity of the starting point of metaphysical inquiry in Descartes and in Avicenna. Both begin with an apodeictic assertion of existence: we have an indubitable intuition of being. As many have remarked, Avicenna's floating man has similarities to Descartes' *cogito*. [46] Avicenna claims that a person floating in the dark, with nothing to see, hear, touch, taste, or smell, still would have a clear intuition of being — of his own existence and the general notion of being. [47] That is, there is indubitable knowledge of existence of your soul, whether or not you have a body or any sense data. [48] Likewise, Descartes claims that, even if we reject all sensory input, we shall still have the certitude of thinking and existing. For both Avicenna and Descartes this certitude, via an intellectual intuition, also known as the light of nature, is absolute, and guarantees our existence *in re*. In contrast, both agree, we may have sensible intuitions of notions like heptagonal houses without such items existing *in re*, but only *in intellectu*. [49]

Descartes and Avicenna have striking similarities of doctrine, and a historical, causal connection, at least indirectly through the writings of Aquinas and later Thomists, is probable.

Newton

Although Descartes and Newton differed on their views of matter, vacuum, and motion, still they shared the view of an infinite space without particular shapes in particular places. Newton's absolute space is a dimensional continuum in which objects, when they move, change the part of space that they occupy.

In his early years at least Newton avoided discussing the metaphysical foundations of his views. Still we do know that he was influenced greatly by Henry More and, through him, by cabalistic writings. [50] The views of the cabalists, Philoponus, the *Kalam*, Avicenna, and the medieval nominalists on space belonged roughly to the same tradition, of rejecting Aristotelian place and advocating an infinite, dimensional continuum. The Mertonian calculators were nominalists, and Newton followed them in thinking about infinitesimals and limits. [51]

The problem for religious and mystics lay in where God, or the prime mover, is to be situated. For after the outermost sphere of the universe there is no container. Such a space then could not be identified with an external containing place, and, with no container, had to be unlimited and infinite. Newton makes similar remarks in the third edition of his *Principia*: God is everywhere. God is not identical to space, but space is that through which God is everywhere. [52] For Newton space is the divine *sensorium*; the space of the universe is finite and has a center, so that there is absolute spatial location; God exists in infinite space outside of the universe. [53]

So Avicenna had a general influence on Newton by his contributions to this tradition, and may have had a more direct influence. There was direct influence of the Islamic materials on seventeenth-century Protestant England via people like the Scalingers. Indeed, an Arabic romance based on the life of Avicenna was translated and popular in England during Newton's time. [54]

Spinoza

Although Spinoza deliberately obliterated his manuscripts and notes on his sources, we do have the advantage of Wolfson's scholarship on what sources Spinoza likely read. In short, Spinoza used works written both in Latin and Hebrew. His two main influences were Cartesian and Judaic philosophers, especially Crescas and Maimonides. [55] We have already seen how Cartesians have been influenced by Avicenna. Suffice it to note then that Crescas and Maimonides were directly influenced by Avicenna. Indeed, many of Avicenna's works had been translated into Hebrew, and, conversely, Jewish philosophers often wrote in Arabic. Being from Spain, Spinoza would have had easy access to Islamic materials.

Like Descartes, Spinoza has a central place for extension, and makes it one of the two divine attributes that we know. By extension Spinoza means an infinite, indivisible dimensional continuum, and argues against those who would make space divisible and finite in place. [56] Wolfson claims that Spinoza is arguing, with Crescas, against Averroës and Aristotle, for the dimensional view of space, which originates with Philoponus and Avicenna. [57]

Note then how for Spinoza extension becomes primary for the existence of substance, and then immediately the issue whether it has the characteristic of divisibility is raised. We have seen a similar progression in Avicenna's account of the coming to be of a thing.

Leibniz

Like Descartes Leibniz was trained scholastically, but, unlike him, portrayed himself as a defender of scholasticism. In particular, he admired Aquinas. [58] So, again, Avicenna could have influenced Leibniz indirectly through Aquinas. Leibniz does cite Avicenna but only rarely, for example, his theory of *cholcodea* for the activity of the soul. [59] Still we do know that Leibniz studied Maimonides' *Guide* and wrote many marginal notes in his copy on the theory of space presented there: the theory of the tradition of the cabalist, the *Kalam*, Philoponus, and Avicenna. [60]

For Leibniz as for Avicenna, the notions of necessary being and possible being are central. Leibniz presents an a priori proof, an ontological argument, from the definition or essence of necessary being. [61] Leibniz also has an a posteriori proof, from the contingent existence of things. Possible beings have their essences and content determined internally. [62] Still, being merely possible, they need an actual cause to exist. That actual cause must exist necessarily, not merely contingently. Hence God, as the necessary being, exists. God does not create things in respect of their essences, but only insofar as certain essences come to exist: ". . . the source of existences but also of essences is in God, insofar as these essences are real or insofar as there is something real in possibility." [63] God then is responsible for the existence but not the essence of things.

All this resembles Avicenna's views. He likewise says that God is responsible for the existence and not the essence of things, and has these two proofs that the necessary being exists. [64] Of course Leibniz need not have gotten this material directly.

Leibniz is commonly credited in his a priori, ontological proof for inserting a missing step into the proof: to show that God is the sort of thing that might exist. [65] Leibniz puts this: God exists if he is possible. [66] That is, the definition of "God" has to be shown consistent, and the divine attributes compossible, before it is asserted that it is possible that God exists. Avicenna also makes this step quite explicitly in his proof of the necessary being. [67]

Kant

Avicenna's views also have some similarities with Kant. Kant of course shares Newton's view of space as a dimensional continuum. [68] More intriguing is the congruence of insight between Avicenna and Kant on the constitution of an object.

It is reasonable to correlate Kant's conception of the analytic, as it is determined by the definition, with what holds on the level of quiddities in themselves; likewise to correlate the synthetic with what holds on the level of quiddities *in re*, where quiddities in different categories are combined. The synthetic a priori then will concern the necessary accidents or *propria*; the synthetic a posteriori the contingent accidents.

Thus far I have merely noted a congruence between the Kantian and the Aristotelian philosophy. But the resemblance of Kant's views to Avicenna's is stronger. In particular, Avicenna's conclusions agree with the examples that Kant commonly gives for synthetic a priori propositions. In Aristotelian terms, such a proposition predicates a *proprium* of its subject: the predication is essential, necessary, and hence a priori, but still not directly contained in the definition, and so not analytic but synthetic. As we have seen, Avicenna says that "a body is three-dimensional" is not true by definition. Rather the predicate, "three-dimensional" is a *proprium* that becomes essential to its subject, "a body," when that quiddity in itself gains material existence. Kant similarly states that that proposition is synthetic a priori. [69] They would likewise agree on the claims that "a body has weight" is synthetic a priori, and "a body is extended" is analytic. [70] So again we have a congruence of doctrine.

By the way, in his discussion of the reality of number, Avicenna insists that "9 + 1 = 10" is necessarily true, not in virtue of the definition by itself, but, synthetically, through a connection of quiddities: "Rather ten is the totality of nine and one, when it is taken as a totality, and then from the two of them there comes to be something different from them." [71] Avicenna would therefore agree with Kant that "7 + 5 = 12" is synthetic. But that is another topic. [72]

Consequently, Kant follows Avicenna not only in general, on the doctrine of space as a dimensional continuum, but also in particular, with respect to which a priori propositions are analytic, and which synthetic. It is difficult, however, to determine the actual historical connections.

Conclusions

Some evidence suggests that Islamic philosophers, especially Avicenna, had considerable influence (perhaps indirectly) on modern philosophy. Further *Quellenforschung* should be fruitful in evaluating the history of philosophy, in particular, specific doctrines of modern philosophers. Despite their affectations of starting *de novo*, modern philosophers too have relied on sources. It is a mistake for scholars in the history of philosophy also to affect the fashion of studying philosophers *de novo*, apart from their antecedents.

Notes

[1] For a fuller exposition of these doctrines, see A. Bäck, "Ibn Sina: The Individuation of Perceptible Substances," *Proceedings of the PMR Conference* 14 (1989), 23-42.

[2] Indeed at *Al-Maqulat*, ed. G. Anawati et al. (Cairo 1959), 115,4-6, Avicenna distinguishes two corporeities, one substantial, one accidental. The substantial corporeity concerns dimensionality; the accidental one the quantitative features of the definite shape. The shape is in the category of quality, 112,11.

[3] *Al-Maqulat* (n. 2), 112,5; 114,1-4. For Avicenna, corporeity is a substance, 112,16-18; that is, body *per se* is substance, 75,19-76,1. Still, substance is fundamentally form plus prime matter, 73,18-19, and prime matter and form are prior to body, 74,10-11. What is *per se* may be either a constituent or a concomitant of the essence, 78,10. So it seems prudent to conclude that for Avicenna corporeity is a *proprium* and not a *genus* of substance.

[4] M. De Wulf, *A History of Medieval Philosophy*, trans. E.C. Messenger (London 1926), II,269, 271.

[5] N. Rescher, "The Impact of Arabic Philosophy on the West," *Studies in Arabic Philosophy* (Pittsburgh 1966), 151-52.

[6] The popularity of Averroës has perhaps two main causes: first, his commentaries on Aristotle that remain faithful to the original text; second, his adherence to the unity of the active intellect. Most of Averroës' points can be found in earlier sources, often in Greek commentators like Alexander and Aphrodisias or in Avicenna himself. To be sure, Averroës was read more than Avicenna. Why have I not written on Averroës instead? Because Avicenna is a more original source.

[7] W.A. Wallace, *Galileo and His Sources* (Princeton 1984), 123. I think it likely that on this issue the knowledge of Avicenna came from Averroës' accounts, since there do not seem to have been available translations of most of the relevant texts of Avicenna.

[8] A.-M. Goichon, *The Philosophy of Avicenna and Its Influence on Medieval Europe*, trans. M. Khan (Delhi 1969), 101.

[9] W.A. Wallace, *Prelude to Galileo* (Dordrecht 1981), 288. See also *The Cambridge History of Renaissance Philosophy* (Cambridge 1988), 209, n. 22.

[10] E.g., *Disputationes* V,ii,23; V,iv,1; here the works seems to be cited more than read.

[11] Dante, *Inferno* IV,143-44; XXVIII,22-63. Rescher (n. 5), 150, incorrectly says "Purgatory."

[12] P. Boyle, *Dante: Philomythes and Philosopher* (Cambridge 1981), 196-97, 247.

[13] Miguel Asin Palacios, *Islam and the Divine Comedy*, trans. and ed. H. Sutherland (London 1968).

[14] E. Rossi, "Quelques contributions à la bibliiographie italienne Avicenne," *Le livre du millenaire d'Avicenne* (Tehran 1956), IV,159-61, lists the many editions of Al-Qanun, in Arabic and in Latin-Hebrew translation, starting in 1491.

[15] In 1446, teaching nominalism was banned at Paris; the ban was lifted in 1481. De Wulf (n. 4), II,287-88.

[16] Buridan, *Subtilissimae quaestiones super octo Physicorum libros Aristotelis*; Albert of Saxony, *Quaestiones in Aristotelis libros Physicorum*; E. Grant, "Place and Space in Medieval Thought," *Motion and Time; Space and Matter*, ed. P. Machamer and R. Turnbull (Columbus 1976), 138.

[17] *Commentaria una cum quaestionibus in octo libros Aristotelis de Physica auscultatione.* Cf. Grant (n. 16), 154. Toletus also published a commentary on the whole of Aristotle's logic and one on Aquinas' *Summa theologiae*.

[18] W.A. Wallace, "Duhem and Koyré on Domingo de Soto," *Synthèse* 83 (1990), 242-51.

[19] Wallace (n. 9), 196, 171, 271-73.

[20] Giordano Bruno, *De la causa, Opera Italiana*, 228, cited in I. Leclerc, *The Nature of Physical Existence* (London 1972), 133-34.

[21] Averroës also had an account of matter with indeterminate dimension. J. Weisheipl, "The Concept of Matter in Fourteenth-Century Science," *The Concept of Matter in Greek and Medieval Philosophy*, ed. E. McMullin (Notre Dame 1963), 154-55, notes a dispute between Averroës and Avicenna on the nature of matter: the former had a view of matter with indeterminate dimensions, while the latter admitted matter with only definite dimensions and an actual quantity. Note that above I have claimed that this is not correct: Avicenna has a Platonist conception of matter as a receptacle prior to dimension; corporeity and matter existing in re have indeterminate dimensions. Cf. H. Wolfson, *The Philosophy of Spinoza* (New York 1959), 235, who agrees with my account. Perhaps Bruno is closer to Averroës here. H. Wolfson and M. Jammer, *Concepts of Space*, 2nd ed. (Cambridge, MA 1969), 89,

suggest a cabalist influence also.

[22] S. Menn, "Descartes and Some Predecessors on the Divine Conservation of Motion," *Synthèse* 33 (1990), 224. On the role of Philoponus, see Wolfson and Jammer (n. 21), 55-57; M. Wolff, "Philoponus and the Rise of Preclassical Dynamics," *Philoponus and the Rejection of Aristotelian Science*, ed. R. Sorabji (Ithaca 1987), 86-87, 91-92.

[23] F. Zimmermann, "Philoponus' Impetus Theory in the Arabic Tradition," *Philoponus and the Rejection of Aristotelian Science*, ed. R. Sorabji (Ithaca 1987), 128-29.

[24] *Al-Ilahiyyat*, ed. G. Anawati et al. (Cairo 1960), 381-93 (= *Metaphysica* [Venice 1508] 102^r,col. 2-103^v,col. 1).

[25] Menn (n. 22), 225.

[26] P. Duhem, "Research on the History of Physical Theories," *Synthèse* 33 (1990), 192.

[27] Ibid, 197.

[28] Menn (n. 22), 235.

[29] Thus, E.-H. Gilson, *Index Scolastico-Cartésienne* (Paris 1912), s.v. "espace," 96, quotes Toletus, and, s.v. "matière," Suarez as scholastic antecedents of Descartes.

[30] C. Normore, "Meaning and Objective Being: Descartes and His Soul," *Essays on Descartes's Meditations*, ed. A. Rorty (Berkeley 1986), 231.

[31] D. Garber, "*Semel in vita*: The Scientific Background in Descartes' *Meditations*," *Essays on Descartes's Meditations* (n. 30), 88

[32] N. Kemp Smith, *New Studies in the Philosophy of Descartes* (New York 1966), 4; E. Gilson, ed. and comm., *Discours de la méthode* (Paris 1925), 103-19. See also R. Ariew, "Descartes and Scholasticism," *The Cambridge Companion to Descartes*, ed. J. Cottingham (Cambridge 1992), 76.

[33] P. Machamer, "Causality and Explanation in Descartes' Natural Philosophy," *Motion and Time; Space and Matter* (n. 16), 172-73; cf. Descartes, *Le monde*, 17, *The Philosophical Writings of Descartes*, trans. J. Cottingham et al. (Cambridge 1984), Vol. 85; rather than "atomist," it might be better to say "particle," as Descartes denies the existence of a vacuum. As I shall note below, it is unclear why

Descartes held an atomist view with conservation of quantitative measure. It is clear that Bruno held this view. See his *De triplici minimo* I,14; Ksenija Atanasijevic, *The Metaphysical and Geometrical Doctrine of Bruno*, trans. G. Tomashevich (St. Louis 1972), 51.

[34] *Principia philosophiae* II,4; II,11; Machamer (n. 33), 172: "Descartes' notion of extension is somewhat unclear. It is identified with the three-dimensional view of body."

In fact, there seems to be considerable disagreement among Cartesian scholars about what theory or theories Descartes did hold. Cf. M. Gueroult, *Spinoza* (Paris 1968), I,529-30, who attributes an "atomist" view to Descartes on space, and claims, 545, that Descartes distinguishes the physical and the mathematical body. For him, 215, Descartes maintains that extension is finite and divisible, whereas Spinoza holds it to be infinite and indivisible. On the other side, Wolfson, *The Philosophy of Spinoza* (n. 21), 268-70, maintains that Descartes holds extension to be infinite and indivisible. As my account does not depend on resolving these issues, I bypass them.

[35] W. Anderson, "Cartesian Motion," *Motion and Time; Space and Matter* (n. 16), 201-02. At *Principia philosophiae* II,11, however, Descartes may be identifying the extension with the particular quantity.

[36] That is, the one that I have attributed to him. Descartes' purported view resembles the view that Weisheipl attributes to Avicenna.

[37] *The Metaphysica of Avicenna,* trans. and comm. P. Morewedge (New York 1970), 17. See also Morewedge's discussion of the wax example, 17, n. 2, and 199-200.

[38] *Al-Ilahiyyat* 64,1-4 (= *Metaphysica* 75^v,col. 1).

[39] *Al-Maqulat* (n. 2), 114,5-10.

[40] *Meditation 2, The Philosophical Writings of Descartes* (n. 33), 20 § 31.

[41] *Meditation 2* (n. 40), 21 § 31.

[42] *Principia philosophiae* I,53.

[43] *Principia philosophiae* II,4. Descartes, like Avicenna, also recognizes the Aristotelian place, and similarly dismisses it as secondary, *Principia philosophiae* II,43.

[44] Descartes, *Objections and Replies* 5,8, in *The Collected Works of Descartes*, II,

248 § 359.

[45] At *Al-Ilahiyyat* 64,16-65,3 (= *Metaphysica* 75^v,col. 1) and Al-Maqulat (n. 2) 115, Avicenna distinguishes the logical and the scientific body. Martial Gue Spinoza, 545, claims the same for Descartes.

[46] Goichon (n. 8), 78.

[47] T. Druart, "The Soul and Body Problem: Avicenna and Descartes," in *Arabic Philosophy and the West*, ed. T. Druart (Washington 1988). M. Marmura, "Avicenna's 'Flying Man' in Context," *The Monist* 69 (1986).

[48] Avicenna, *De anima* 2^v,col. 2; 27^r,col. 2. This hypothesis is, in effect, the sensory deprivation tank; recent research contradicts Avicenna's claim: the person will just lose consciousness.

[49] *Al-Ilahiyyat* 195,7-10 (= *Metaphysica* 86^v,col. 1). In *Meditation 6*, Descartes likewise separates the powers of cognition and imagination in discussing knowledge of the *chiliagon*.

[50] Wolfson and Jammer (n. 21), 111-12, 41-48.

[51] Grant (n. 16), 161.

[52] *Philosophiae naturalis principia mathematica*, ed. A. Koyré and I.B. Cohen (Cambridge, MA 1972), II,528(20)-529(10) [760-62].

[53] Wolfson and Jammer (n. 21), 113-15, discuss Newton's concept of the divine *sensorium*.

[54] Rescher (n. 5), 153-54.

[55] Wolfson, *The Philosophy of Spinoza* (n. 21), 8-9, 13, 19.

[56] *Ethics* I,15 S.

[57] Wolfson, *The Philosophy of Spinoza* (n. 21), 268-70, 275; idem, *Cresca's Critique of Aristotle* (Cambridge 1919), 187. Wolfson says, as noted in n. 33: not against Descartes.

[58] *Discourse on Metaphysics* 3, 11

[59] "On Nature Itself," trans. L. Loemker, in *Philosophical Paper Letters*, 2 vols. (Chicago 1956), 810. Cf. T. Gaskill, "Was Leibniz an Avicennean?," *Proceedings of*

the PMR Conference 16\17 (1992-1993), 108.

60 Wolfson and Jammer (n. 21), 64.

61 *Discourse on Metaphysics* 23; *Monadology* 45.

62 *Monadology* 11, 46-47.

63 *Monadology* 43.

64 *Ilahiyyat* 38,11-6 (= *Metaphysica* 73^r,col. 2); 46,6-9 (= 74^r,col. 1]; 257,7
260,9-11; 261,10-1; 262,12-4 (= 91^r,col. 2-91^v,col. 2). See A. Bäck, "Avicenna's
Conception of the Modalities," *Vivarium* 30, No. 2 (1992), 241-46.

65 E.g., N. Malcolm, "Anselm's Ontological Arguments," *The Many Argument*,
eds. J. Hick and A. McGill (New York 1967), 317-18.

66 *Discourse on Metaphysics* 23; *Monadology* 45; *New Essays* IV,7

67 *Al-Ilahiyyat* 346,8 (= *Metaphysica* 99^r,col. 1).

68 However they differ somewhat on the ontological status of space. R. Palter,
"Absolute Space and Absolute Motion," *Proceedings of Third International Kant
Congress*, ed. L.W. Beck (Dordrecht 1969), 177; and R. Butts, "On Buchdahl's and
Palter's Papers," *Proceedings of Third International Kant Congress*, ed. L.W. Beck
(Dordrecht 1969), 196-97.

69 *Critique of Pure Reason* B41; *Prolegomena* § 12.

70 *Critique of Pure Reason* B41; *Prolegomena* § 12.

71 *Al-Ilahiyyat* 121,7-8 (= *Metaphysica* 80^v,col. 1); Kant, *Critique of Pure Reason*
B15; *Prolegomena* § 2c2.

72 Avicenna would also probably agree that "every event has a cause" is synthetic a priori. (Kant, *Critique* B5; B13; *Prolegomena* § 15). For he demands that
every contingent being have an external cause. One possible counter example is
Kant's claim that "gold is a yellow metal" is analytic (*Prolegomena* § 26). For color
is an accidental quality for Avicenna, and so the proposition would not be a priori at
all.

II

Prolegomena to the Voyage

Arabic Astronomy
during the Age of Discovery

George Saliba

Introduction

The Age of Discovery may be taken to fall between 1415, when the Portuguese captured Ceuta (Sebta) on the North African Coast, and 1642, when New Zealand was discovered. [1] To most students of Arabic science, this age, so celebrated in the Latin West for its exuberance and wealth, is an age of decline in the lands of Islam.

In accounts of Islamic intellectual history, historians assign "golden" and "not-so golden" ages to various periods. For example, the ninth and tenth centuries are often cited as the golden age of Islamic science, [2] or even as the age of rationalism. According to this classification, that golden age began to wane toward the end of the eleventh, or beginning of the twelfth centuries, with the Ash'arite theologian Abu Hamid al-Ghazzali († 1111). Ghazzali supposedly dealt the age a fatal blow by writing his *Tahafut al-Falasifah*, commonly translated as the *Incoherence of the Philosophers*. And it is commonly held that Averroës' († 1198) response to Ghazzali the *Tahafut al-Tahafut*, the *Incoherence of the Incoherence*, was the last gasp of rationalism. [3] After that blow the whole intellectual structure of Islamic civilization supposedly crumbled under the resurgence of an Islamic religious fanaticism, intolerant of rational activity in general, and science in particular. Edward Sachau, a most celebrated German orientalist, worked more than most to introduce the achievements of Islamic science to the West. Expressing his chagrin, Sachau said about that downturn of Islamic civilization:

> The fourth century [of the Islamic calendar, i.e. the tenth in the Christian calendar] is the turning point in the history of the spirit of Islam, and the establishment of the orthodox faith about five hundred sealed the fate of independent research for ever. But for Alash'ari and Alghazzali the Arabs might have been a nation of Galileos, Keplers, and Newtons. [4]

If Sachau is correct, any discussion of Arabic astronomy during the Age of Discovery would be a futile attempt to patch together a few intellectual achievements amounting to nothing. And yet, I claim, the study of Arabic science during that so-called period of "decline" overturns the commonly-held opinion in every scientific discipline, from mechanics to astronomy, from physics to medicine, from mathematics to trigonometry. In the field of astronomy in particular, I assert, the achievements wrought by astronomers, writing mainly in Arabic in every corner of the Islamic world, were as ingenious and sophisticated as their counterparts in late Medieval and Renaissance Europe. As recent research on Copernican astronomy demonstrates, Copernican astronomy can only be properly understood through reference to Arabic astronomy. [5]

The focus in this study is on Arabic astronomy during the Age of Discovery, without consideration of such distinguished scientists as Jazari (c. 1206) [6] in mechanics, Nasir al-Din al-Tusi († 1274) [7] in trigonometry, Ibn al-Nafis (c. 1288) [8] in medicine, and Kamal al-Din al-Farisi (c. 1320) [9] in optics, all of whom lived during the so-called age of decline and whose works are not as yet popularly known.

As regards astronomy, the beginning of the Age of Discovery coincides almost exactly with the establishment (c. 1420) of the famous Islamic observatory founded by the Central Asian potentate and astronomer Ulugh Beg (1393-1449), the grandson of Tamerlane (1369-1405). [10] This observatory, built in the Central Asian city of Samarqand, was modeled after the observatory built in Maragha in northwest Iran, during Ilkhanid rule, toward the middle thirteenth century. These observatories reached their zenith during the so-called age of decline.

By the beginning of the Age of Discovery, astronomical activity in the lands of Islam continued its age-long tradition, with no sign of decline. In fact, the sixteenth century witnessed remarkable development in theoretical astronomy, where planetary theories advanced through the use of mathematics to describe celestial phenomena.

Toward the beginning of the Age of Discovery, Ulugh Beg added a school to his observatory at Samarqand which attracted creative scientific minds to its faculty. [12] One participant, Jamshid b. Ghiyath al-Din al-Kashi († 1429), left a report about activities at the school in a letter to his father. This letter, published by the Turk, Aydin Sayili, informs us of personalities involved in the construction of astronomical instruments, the teaching of mathematical science, and the scientific environment. [13] The letter makes it clear that Ulugh Beg was not only a patron of astronomy, but an astronomer himself. According to Kashi's letter, Ulugh Beg used to deliver lectures on the two most advanced astronomical works of his time, namely the *Tadhkira* of the same Nasir al-Din al-Tusi, and the *Tuhfa* of Tusi's student Qutb al-Din al-Shirazi (†1311). [14] Other contemporary sources, such as 'Ala' al-Din al-Qushji (†1474), who studied under Ulugh Beg himself, and Fathallah al-Shirwani (†1486) [15], a product of the school, confirm Ulugh Beg's actual participation and patronization.

Thus, the Persian handbook of astronomy, *Zij-i Sultani Gurgani*, [16] is in all likelihood Ulugh Beg's personal production, or at the very least the result of his active collaboration with his students and colleagues. The material covered in this sophisticated handbook clearly represents original astronomy pursued at that observatory. Accordingly, for the last three hundred years, this handbook has attracted the attention of European astronomers and orientalists such as Hyde, Flamsteed, Greaves, and Sedillot, and has continued to be used by astronomers down to this century. [17] Information regarding this handbook can be obtained elsewhere. [18]

General Considerations

Around the twelfth century, instead of the death of astronomical activity, an actual restructuring of astronomy as a scientific discipline took place. The new astronomy, cleansed of religiously-condemned astrology, was incorporated into acceptable intellectual Islamic thought. [19] The *muwaqqit*, ostensibly the time keeper of religious practices, but now also a student of planetary theory, became part of mosque bureaucracy, allowed to work within the bosom of the Muslim community. David King of Frankfurt University has attested to this fact, and demonstrated the spread of this new astronomy in the later medieval centuries under the rubric of the religiously-condoned science of *'ilm al-miqat*. [20]

With this reconstruction, astronomy was divided into various branches: (1) *'ilm al-hay'a*, theoretical astronomy dealing with planetary theories, a discipline that shared some of the problems with, but had no exact parallel in Greek astronomy; (2) *'ilm al-miqat*, timekeeping; and *(3) 'ilm al-azyaj*, which dealt with manipulation of ephemerids commonly preserved in such astronomical handbooks as Ulugh Beg's. Among others subdivisions, the field of astronomical instruments (which continued to flourish after the twelfth century, and well into the age of decline) should also be included.

At this time, astronomical research focussed on universal application. A prime example is the astrolabe. This astronomical instrument was limited only by the number of plates it could accommodate, inasmuch as each geographical locality required a different and specific plate. The theory behind the instrument was Greek, but its development was Islamic. During the so-called period of decline, the astrolabe was adapted for universal applicability in any geographical locale. [21]

The complicated calculation of the direction of Mecca from any specific geographical location led to further developments. [22] In order to solve such problems of spherical trigonometry, tables containing thousands of entries giving the direction of Mecca from any geographical locale were computed. [23] Similarly, simplification of the use of ephemerids was so advanced during these same centuries that, by the end of the fifteenth century, all they required was the mastery of elementary addition. [24] By contrast, the classical *Handy Tables* of Ptolemy for the same purpose appear unduly complex. As the works of the seventeenth-century Qazwini demonstrate, the mosque astronomers, the *muwaqqits*, were manipulating mathematical functions with ease. [25]

Most importantly, once the new astronomy had religious approval, introduction not only into the mosque, but also into the *madrasa*, the main educational institution of pre-modern Islam, followed. [26] In fact, evidence indicates that *hay'a* texts, dealing with planetary theories, were still taught in the traditional *madrasas* of Iran until the beginning of the twentieth century. [27]

Developments in Theoretical Astronomy

Fifteenth-century Islamic theoretical astronomy demonstrated a degree of sophistication, and a level of achievement, barely begun in the eleventh and twelfth centuries and continuing through the age of "decline" well into the Age of Discovery. Islamic astronomers continually criticized the traditional Ptolemaic astronomy, and finally succeeded in showing its inadequacy. [28] Incidentally, similar motivation ultimately led Copernicus to propose his own astronomy, [29] identical in many respects to the novel astronomies proposed in the Islamic East three centuries before Copernicus. [30]

The full significance of these developments can be appreciated only by a comparison with the traditional Ptolemaic astronomy. According to Ptolemy, the sun moved annually around the earth. Conversely, according to Copernicus, the earth moved annually around the sun. Either theory could account for the phenomena — without loss in mathematical rigor: [31] it makes no mathematical difference whether the earth or the sun is the center around which these motions take place.

For an observer on earth, the apparent yearly motion of the sun around us — which produces the unequal seasons — can be explained, according to Ptolemy, in one of two ways. If we assume (fig. 1) that we are at point Q, then we can either say that the body of the sun revolves around us along a circle ABG, whose center is slightly removed from the earth in the direction of the apogee A, or that the body of the sun moves around the periphery of a small solid sphere, called the epicycle, which is itself carried by another larger sphere, called the deferent, whose center is identical to that of the earth. Both Apollonius and Ptolemy had already demonstrated that when the epicycle is allowed to move at the same but apposite speed as the deferent, and if the radius of the epicycle is equal to the eccentricity of circle *ABG*, then both models, the eccentric as well as the epicyclic, could account equally well for the apparent motion of the sun across the seasons.

Now, if we assume the path left by the center of the epicycle as it moves around the earth as sufficient to represent the sphere that carries the epicycle, and if we represent the epicycle by a simple circle, then the following diagram (fig. 2), used by Ptolemy in *Almagest* III,3, would illustrate more simply the two alternative models, the eccentric and the epicyclic. The observer is still at point *Q*, and the sun could move either around its own circle *ABG*, whose center is not identical with that of the earth and is displaced in the direction of the apogee, or around the epicycle whose center moves, in turn, along a concentric circle. By simple geometry, one can demonstrate that the final path of the solar body in the epicyclic alternative model will coincide with the eccentric circle. This Ptolemaic model of the sun did not meet any objection throughout medieval astronomy, except in one instance where it was found that it did not account properly for the variation in the apparent solar disk at the time of eclipses. [32]

The model for the upper planets (fig. 3), namely Saturn, Jupiter, Mars, and the planet Venus, is similar to this one, except for the addition of a slight modification. Now the deferent itself is eccentric and is carried by a concentric inclined sphere. Just as in the case of the solar model, we take the path of the epicyclic center to be a circle representing the eccentric deferent and simplify the model by representing it with circles only as in the *Almagest* (fig. 4). In this simplified model, for an observer, who is still situated at point *Q*, the planet seems to be moving around its own epicycle, now represented as a circle with center *Z*, and the epicyclic center *Z* itself is moved by the eccentric deferent with center *T*. This would have been acceptable, if the deferent sphere were to move uniformly around its own center *T*, thus satisfying the basic Greek philosophical axiom of uniform circular motion to which Ptolemy was supposed to adhere. Instead, we note in this model that the diameter of the epicycle from which the epicycle's own motion is measured points neither to the center of the universe, nor to the center of the deferent, but rather to a third point called the equant, here designated as *D*. This feature of Ptolemy's model is none other than the notorious equant, which every astronomer worth his name — including Copernicus — attempted to explain away. In a nutshell, Ptolemy proposed a model in which the solid sphere of the deferent is supposed to move uniformly around an axis which does not pass through its center — a physical impossibility.

The main contribution of Arabic astronomy after the eleventh century, that is, during the period of decline, was a series of attempts to remedy this situation. Accepting the given axiom of circular uniform motion, and accepting the Ptolemaic observations as true, Arabic astronomers then represented the physical universe (together with its axioms) by mathematical models that could account for observed phenomena. Astronomy, as a science, had to be consistent. This same methodology was expressed by Copernicus in the *Commentariolus*. [33] Various astronomers such as Mu'ayyad al-Din al-'Urdi († 1266), Nasir al-Din al-Tusi († 1274), and Ibn al-Shatir († 1375) all attempted to solve this specific problem. [34]

'Urdi's solution (fig. 5) of the equant problem rests on the notion of bisecting the Ptolemaic eccentricity at point *K*, and compensating for this bisection with a small epicyclet with center *N* carried at the circumference of the newly devised deferent. 'Urdi then proposed a new mathematical lemma which allowed him to prove that, by allowing the appropriate motions to take place, the new center of the epicycle according to his own model, namely point *O*, will not only fall very close to the Ptolemaic epicyclic center *Z* (the difference is exaggerated here for our convenience but could not possibly be perceptible on a diagram of this size), but also will fall along a line *OD* which is proven to be invariably parallel to line *KN*. Now, since the new deferent with center *K* moves uniformly around its own center *K*, and the little epicyclet with center *N* moves also uniformly around its own center *N*, then the resultant motion of *O* would violate neither the axioms nor the observations if the resultant motion of *O* turned out to move uniformly around point *D*, the equant.

'Urdi's newly devised mathematical lemma (fig. 6) does indeed demonstrate such uniform motion. The same theorem was also used by Copernicus to solve the same equant problem. Similarly, when Kepler wrote to his teacher Maestlin requesting the explanation of this very feature in Copernican astronomy, Maestlin replied with what amounts to the same proof of the 'Urdi Lemma. [35] This similarity leaves very little doubt about the identity of the mathematical techniques used first by 'Urdi before 1266, and then by Copernicus in the early part of the sixteenth century.

Tusi also proposed his own solution to the problem, another mathematical theorem (fig. 7), now called the Tusi Couple. If one takes two spheres, tangent internally at one point, one of them being half the size of the other, and if one allows the bigger sphere to move at any angle, and the small sphere to move by twice that angle in the opposite direction, then the point of tangency, which was on the circumference of the small sphere, will move along a straight line that passes through the center of the larger sphere. This combination allows circular motions to be translated into linear motions and vice versa. In modern mathematical terminology, the Tusi Couple allows a vector to rotate at uniform speed while its length is shortened and elongated as it revolves. More dramatically, as Hartner noted some twenty years ago, the Tusi Couple does indeed upset the neat Aristotelian distinction between linear and circular motions, where according to Aristotle circular motion is reserved for celestial bodies only, by demonstrating that one of these motions could easily result from the other. [36]

For theoretical astronomy, this theorem allowed Tusi to preserve the Ptolemaic observations, and to modify the Ptolemaic model by adding a Tusi Couple within the thickness of a new deferent (fig. 8), centered on point D, such that the Ptolemaic epicyclic center will be carried at the point of tangency of the Tusi Couple, which could now oscillate along a straight line. Once the appropriate motions are prescribed, the Ptolemaic epicycle could then be brought close to point D and removed away from it in order to describe the Ptolemaic deferent, without sacrificing its uniform motion around its new center D. Like that of 'Urdi, this arrangement too could solve the equant problem in the Ptolemaic model. Copernicus also used a Tusi Couple in his *De revolutionibus*, and applied it to the Mercury model. This third modification of the Ptolemaic model was introduced by Ibn al-Shatir of Damascus († 1375) [37] and contained the same elements as the Copernican model except for the heliocentricity, which is at this stage mathematically trivial.

Khafri's Model for the Upper Planets

During the Age of Discovery, all those solutions were available to Islamic astronomers. In fact, 'Urdi's Lemma and the Tusi Couple may have also become available in the Latin West by the early part of the Age of Discovery. [38] A relatively unknown author, Shams al-Din al-Khafri (c. 1522), a contemporary of Copernicus, was aware of these previous attempts to modify the Ptolemaic models. After discussing the virtues of each modification, and demonstrating their mathematical equivalence, Khafri went on to say that he too could still add his own modification. [39] His approach to this problem and the modification of the Mercury model exhibit Khafri's full realization that these questions do not have unique mathematical solutions. In fact, the sheer number of proposed solutions demonstrates the power of mathematics to represent celestial phenomena otherwise difficult to describe.

Khafri solves the problem by introducing two new eccentrics instead of the Ptolemaic deferent. (fig. 9) The first eccentric is centered at point *K*, while the second is centered at *K'*. If the first eccentric moves in the direction of the signs by an angle 2α, which is equal to twice the Ptolemaic mean motion angle, and if the second eccentric moves in the opposite direction by half as much, that is, by the amount of the mean motion only, then line *K'C"* will always be parallel to line *EC*, where *C* is the center of the Ptolemaic epicycle. In order to translate the point *C"* to the position *C'''*, thus making it coincide with the Ptolemaic position, Khafri employs one of two possibilities: either a large epicyclet whose radius is equal to the Ptolemaic eccentricity and moving at the same speed as the second eccentric, but in the opposite direction, or two small epicyclets, each being half the larger one, so fixed with respect to each other that the first one moves at the same speed as the second eccentric, but in the opposite direction, while the other remains fixed along the radius *C"C'''*. Needless to say, Khafri's model employs the same 'Urdi Lemma.

Those four solutions of the equant problem were all produced during the so-called age of decline, and they all had some bearing on the mathematical tools used at the end of that period by Copernicus, whether in the deployment of 'Urdi's Lemma or the Tusi Couple. Those were, however, solutions of a relatively simple problem.

Qushji's Model for Mercury

Reference to the Ptolemaic model for Mercury is necessary to explain modifications imposed on it by the fifteenth-century astronomer, 'Ala' al-Din al-Qushji (†1474). For Ptolemy (fig. 10), the observer, placed at point *O*, will see the planet Mercury *P* as if it is moving on an epicycle with center *C*, while that epicycle is carried by a deferent whose center is *F*. Note that in this model the deferent does not move uniformly around its own center *F*, nor around the center of the world *O*, but rather around a third fictitious point, similar to that used for the upper planets, namely the equant *E*. This model, like other planetary models, also violates the axiom of uniform motion, supposedly acceptable to Ptolemy.

The challenge, therefore, was to devise a model where all motions of the spheres would take place around an axis passing through their centers, and still satisfy the observational conditions stated by Ptolemy and accepted as true by later astronomers. 'Ala' al-Din al-Qushji, a student and protege of Ulugh Beg, responded with a short treatise devoted to the solution of this problem. His introduction tells us that he had a personal relationship with Ulugh Beg and studied mathematics under him. [40]

In Qushji's model (fig. 11), the observer is again placed at the center of the world *O*. The old Ptolemaic director is now replaced by a new one with center *N*, instead of *M*. This new director moves around its own center at the same speed as the Ptolemaic director, thus making lines *MA* always parallel to *NA'*. The deferent moves uniformly, around its own new center *H*, in the opposite direction, at twice that speed. This deferent also carries a small epicyclet with center *B*, which moves at the same speed and in the same direction as the deferent. The small epicyclet itself carries a second epicyclet, with center *D*, which moves at half the speed of the first and in the opposite direction. By taking the two epicyclets to be equal in size, and the diameter of each of them equal to the Ptolemaic eccentricity, the resultant motions, which all take place in strict conformity with the uniform motion axiom, will produce a point *G*, which will be close to point *C*, the Ptolemaic center of the epicycle. (The difference between points *C* and *G* is intentionally exaggerated here to distinguish the two points.)

The use of computers to calculate the differences between the models of Qushji and Ptolemy found that the maximum angular variation for an observer situated at the center of the world will not exceed five minutes of arc, a value which is well within the tolerance of medieval observational devices. At critical points, however, that is, at the apogee and the two perigees whence the Ptolemaic model was derived, the two models yield identical results. Qushji's model meets the theoretical as well as the observational requirements, while not suffering the pitfalls of the Ptolemaic model.

General Assessment and Contacts with Europe

Thus, designation of the twelfth to the fourteenth centuries as a period of decline in Islamic science is far from factual. Indeed, some of the results achieved at that time, at least in regard to theoretical astronomy, are no less sophisticated than their European counterparts. Transmission of these results from East to West and their use by Copernicus is also possible. Parallels exist between mathematical tools used by Copernicus in the sixteenth century and those of Islamic astronomers some two to three centuries earlier. As for the routes of such transmission, Neugebauer pointed to a Byzantine Greek text describing the Tusi Couple, to be found in Italy toward the beginning of the sixteenth century before Copernicus' arrival there. Copernicus may not have actually inspected this text and learned of the Tusi Couple from it. But contacts between the two worlds were definitely occurring at that time. No similar route has as yet been found for the transmission of 'Urdi's Lemma.

The development of the astrolabe illustrates such East-West contacts. In Renaissance Italy, circa 1520, the Florentine architect, Antonio da Sangallo the Younger, to whom we owe the building of the greater part of St. Peter's Basilica, made drawings of an astrolabe. [41] Those drawings were excellent copies of a ninth-century astrolabe made by the Baghdadi astrolabist Khafif *ghulam* (the apprentice) of 'Ali b. 'Isa (c. 850). The original ninth-century astrolabe must have made its way to Italy via medieval Spain. Such interest in Islamic scientific material was expressed by Sangallo that he reproduced in the drawings even the Arabic inscriptions without knowing a word of Arabic. Khafif's was not the best of Islamic astrolabes; yet it was found interesting enough to be copied.

Contact was also occurring in the opposite direction, that is, from West to East, especially after the *Reconquista* and the expulsion of Muslims and Jews from Spain. While neither European books translated into Arabic in their entirety during this period, nor full descriptions of the latest theories prevalent in Europe of the time, such as the Copernican system, have been found, we encounter stray remarks illustrating the intellectual level of the West to East contact. On the fly leaf of an Arabic copy of the *Almagest*, the Ottoman astronomer, Taqi al-Din, (1520-1585), remarks: "As for the *Almagest*, it means the greatest in their language. I have read that in the book of Ambrose Calepino." This remark may refer to the multilingual dictionary of Ambrogio da Calepino (1435-1511), apparently published in 1584 under the title *Dictionarium octo linguarum*, but known to Taqi al-Din before that date. Such a dictionary was probably carried along by the fleeing Muslims and Jews to Constantinople, where it caught the attention of Taqi al-Din.

The scientific traditions of the East did not disappear after the sixteenth century, but continued to fuel research up to the end of the Age of Discovery. The title page of the Latin translation of Ibn al-Haytham's Arabic treatise on the elevation of the pole, by Golios, is clearly marked as completed in 1643. [42] Neither the most sophisticated of Ibn al-Haytham's works, nor representative of innovative trends in Arabic astronomy, this treatise was nevertheless of interest to Europeans as late as mid-seventeenth century.

Conclusion

This survey of achievement in Arabic astronomy during the Age of Discovery should put to rest some well entrenched myths regarding Arabic science and the interaction between Europe and Islam. As to theoretical astronomy, the period after the twelfth century was not one of decline — results still being realized between 1415 and 1642. The accomplishments listed here were extracted from manuscripts scattered throughout modern-day Islam; none of them has as yet been published in its entirety nor translated into any European language. Most of these facts have been garnered sporadically. This brief resume surely represents only the tip of the iceberg, with more and similar results still to be found in thousands of unstudied manuscripts.

Finally, contact between East and West should not be limited to the renascence of the twelfth century. Transmission of science continued well into the Renaissance. The dependence of Copernican astronomy on its Islamic antecedents, exciting and challenging as that may be, is only one example of interaction between these two cultures. This study may serve as a beacon for systematic research. Proper understanding of both the history and roots of Western science will show Arabic contributions elegantly interwoven into contemporary scientific achievement.

Notes

[1] This is the most common meaning of the phrase. See *The Columbia History of the World*, ed. J. Garraty and P. Gay (New York 1972; repr. 1986), 619-20.

[2] See, for example, M. Meyerhof, "Science and Medicine," *The Legacy of Islam*, ed. T. Arnold and A. Guillaume (Oxford 1931), 311-55.

[3] See, for example, F.C. Copleston, *A History of Medieval Philosophy* (London 1972), 124, and J. Weinberg, *A Short History of Medieval Philosophy* (Princeton 1964), 139.

[4] C.E. Sachau, *The Chronology of Ancient Nations: An English Version of the Arabic Text of the Athar-ul-Bakiya of Albiruni* (London 1879), x.

[5] See, for example, my recent article, "The Astronomical Tradition of Maragha: A Historical Survey and Prospects for Future Research," *Arabic Sciences and Philosophy* 1 (1991), 67-99; idem, "Arabic Astronomy and Copernicus," *Zeitschrift für Geschichte der Arabisch-Islamischen Wissenschaft* 1 (1984), 73-87; E.S. Kennedy, et al., *Studies in the Islamic Exact Sciences* (Beirut 1983), 50-107; and N. Swerdlow and O. Neugebauer, *Mathematical Astronomy in Copernicus's De Revolutionibus* (New York 1984), esp. 295.

[6] D. Hill, *The Book of Knowledge of Ingenious Mechanical Devices*, an annotated translation of al-Jazari's book on Mechanics, (Boston 1974).

[7] Nasir al-Din al-Tusi, *Traité de Quadrilatère*, ed., trans. A.P. Caratheodory, (Constantinople 1891).

[8] A.Z. Iskandar, "Ibn al-Nafis," *Dictionary of Scientific Biography* (New York 1974), IX, 603-06. For a discussion of his discovery of the pulmonary circulation of the blood, see the bibliography cited in Iskandar's article, and A. Chéhadé, "Ibn al-Nafis et la découverte de la circulation pulmonaire," M.D. dissertation (Faculté de Médicine, Paris, 1951), no. 1143.

[9] R. Rashed, "Kamal al-Din al-Farisi," *Dictionary of Scientific Biography* (New York 1973), VII,212-19.

[10] Aydin Sayili, *The Observatory in Islam* (Ankara 1960), 260ff.

[11] Ibid., 189-223.

[12] Ibid, 268, et passim.

[13] Aydin Sayili, *Ghiyâth al Dîn al Kâshî's Letter on Ulugh Beg and the Scientific Activity in Samarqand* (Ankara 1985).

[14] Ibid., 59, 95.

[15] For a description of the activities at the Samarqand School, and the involvement of Ulugh Beg in those activities, see *Sharh al-Tadhkira* by Fathallah Shirwani, Süleymeniye Ms. Damat Ibrahim 847, fol. 14^v, et passim.

[16] L.-P.-E. Armelie Sedillot, *Prolégomenes des tables astronomiques d'Oloug-Beg* (Paris 1847-53).

[17] The most recent publication dealing with the star tables of this Zij is that of E. Ball Knobel, *Ulugh Beg's Catalogue of Stars*, the Carnegle Institution of Washlngton, (Washington 1917).

[18] See also the article on Ulugh Beg in the *Dictionary of Scientific Biography* (New York 1970-78).

[19] G. Saliba, "The Development of Astronomy in Medieval Islamic Society," *Arab Studies Quarterly* 4 (1982), 211-25, esp. 225.

[20] See, for example, articles IX-XII in D. King, *Islamic Mathematical Astronomy* (London 1986).

[21] See, for example, D. King, "Universal Solutions to Problems of Spherical Astronomy from Mamluk Egypt and Syria," *A Way Prepared: Essays on Islamic Culture in Honor of Richard Bayly Winder*, ed. F. Kazemi and R. McChesney (New York 1988), 153-84.

[22] See D. King, "Kibla," *Encyclopedia of Islam*, new edition.

[23] See King (n. 20), articles XI, XIII.

[24] See G. Saliba,"The Double Argument Lunar Tables of Cyriacus," *Journal for the History of Astronomy* 7 (1976), 41-46; idem, "Computation of Islamic Astronomical Tables In the Late Middle Ages," [Arabic] *Proceedings of the First International Symposium for the History of Arabic Science* (Aleppo 1976), 275-94; idem, "Computational Techniques in a Set of Late Medieval Astronomical Tables," *Journal for the History of Arabic Science* 1 (1977), 22-32; idem, "The Planetary Tables of Cyriacus," *Journal for the History of Arabic Science* 2 (1978), 53-65; King (n. 20), article V.

[25] Saliba (n. 24), "Tables of Cyriacus" and idem (n. 24) , "Computational

Techniques" (n. 24).

[26] See, G. Saliba, "Persian Scientists in the Islamic World: Astronomy from Maragha to Samarqand" (forthcoming).

[27] Ibid.

[28] For a brief survey of these activities and the direction of future research, see Saliba (n. 5).

[29] See, for example, N. Swerdlow, "The Derivation and First Draft of Copernicus's Planetary Theory: A Translation of the *Commentariolus* with Commentary," *Proceedings of the American Philosophical Society* 117 (1973), 423-512, esp. 434.

[30] Cf. the literature cited in n. 5 above.

[31] For a discussion of the relative motions and the equivalence between the motion of the earth and the motion of the sun see, for example, A. Berry, *A Short History of Astronomy from Earliest Times through the Nineteenth Century* (London 1898; repr. Dover, 1961), 102-03, and O. Neugebauer, *Exact Sciences in Antiquity* (Providence 1957), 122-24

[32] For a discussion of this objection and the alternate model proposed by Ibn al-Shatir of Damascus, see G. Saliba, "Theory and Observation in Islamic Astronomy: the Work of Ibn al-Shatir of Damascus († 1375)," *Journal for the History of Astronomy* 18 (1987), 35-43. Because of observed annular eclipses, there were also some systematic objections to Ptolemy's statement that the apparent solar disk did not vary in size, and was always equal to the apparent disk of the moon when the moon is at its farthest distance from the earth.

[33] See Swerdlow (n. 29), 434.

[34] See Saliba (n. 5).

[35] See A. Grafton, "Michael Maestlin's Account of Copernican Planetary Theory," *Proceedings of the American Philosophical Society* 117 (1973), 523-50, esp. 527-28.

[36] W. Hartner, "Copernicus, the Man, the Work, and its History," *Proceedings of the American Philosophical Society* 117 (1973), 413-22, esp. 416-17. I disagree with Hartner's claim that neither Tusi nor anyone after him noticed that the Tusi Couple disrupts the Aristotelian scheme. See my article: "Some Philosophical Considerations in Arabic Astronomy" (forthcoming).

37 See Swerdlow (n. 29).

38 See Swerdlow and Neugebauer (n. 5).

39 The source for this and the following statement is Khafri's *al-Takmila fi Sharh al-Tadhkira*, Zahiriya Ms. No. 6782, fols. 193^v-194^r.

40 See G. Saliba, "Al-Qushji's Reform of the Ptolemaic Model for Mercury," *Arabic Sciences and Philosophy* 3 (1993), 161-203.

41 See, G. Saliba, "A Sixteenth-Century Drawing of an Astrolabe Made by Khafif Ghulam 'Ali b. 'Isa (c. A.D. 850)," *Nuncius* 6 (1991), 109-119.

42 British Museum Ms. Add. 3034. dated 1646.

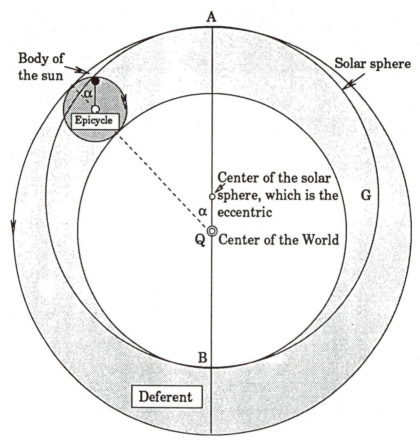

Figure 1
For an observer at the center of the World, the sun appears
as if it is either moved by its own eccentric sphere, here designated
by the circle *ABG*, or is moved by an epicycle which is itself carried
by a deferent concentric with the center of the world.

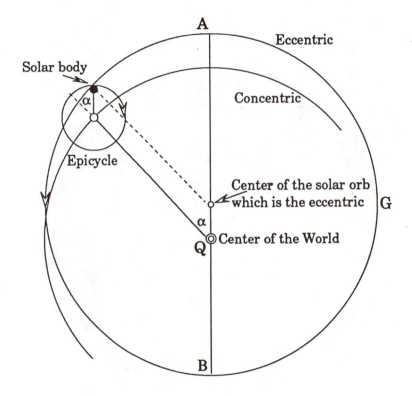

Figure 2
The equivalence of the eccentric and the epicyclic models as
presented in the *Almagest*, with circles representing the
previous solid spheres.

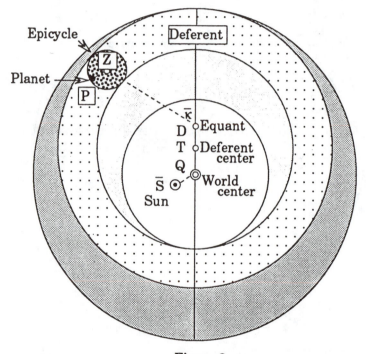

Figure 3
Ptolemy's model for the upper planets represented in solid
spheres as he imagined it and as it was imagined by Medieval
and Renaissance astronomers.

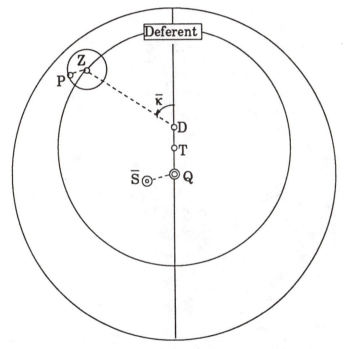

Figure 4
Ptolemy's model for the upper planets where solid
spheres are represented by simpler circles.

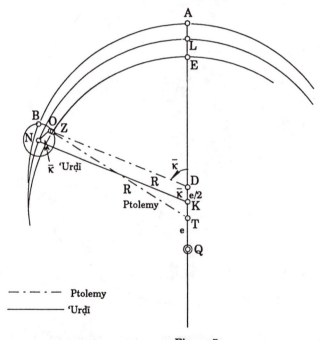

Figure 5
'Urḍī's modification of Ptolemy's model. According to 'Urḍī's model, the
obsrever is still at Q, but the epicycle now has a center O which is very close to
the Ptolemaic center Z. 'Urḍī's Lemma allows O to rotate around N, and N to
rotate around K at the same speed thus making O look as if it is rotating
around the Equant D at the same speed.

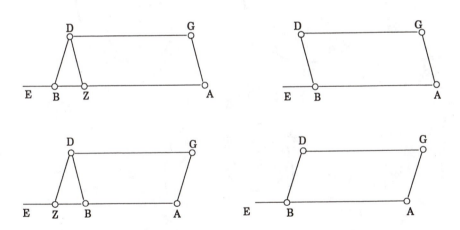

Figure 6
'Urḍī's Lemma. If any two equal lines AG, BD, describe equal angles with
respect to line AB, whether internally or externally, then line GD, which joins
the extremities of the two said lines will always be parallel to line AB.

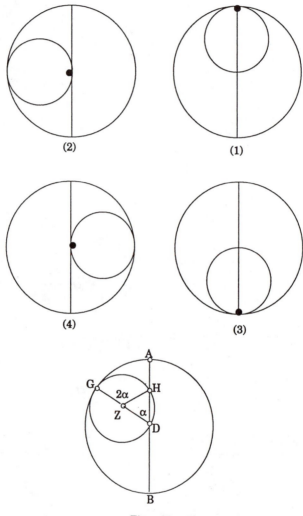

Figure 7

The Ṭūsī Couple. As the big sphere moves by an angle α,
and the small sphere moves in the opposite direction by an
angle 2α, the common point H will oscillate back and forth
along diameter AB. Hartner drew attention to the
similarities between the lettering used by Copernicus and
that used by Ṭūsī to prove the same theorem.

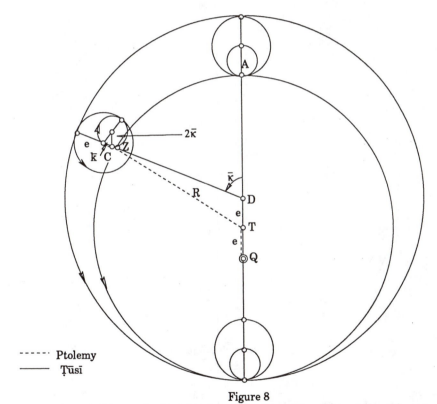

Figure 8

Ṭūsī's model uses the Ṭūsī Couple to allow the radius of the sphere with center D to oscillate in length thus duplicating the Ptolemaic deferent at the same speed as the Ptolemaic deferent.

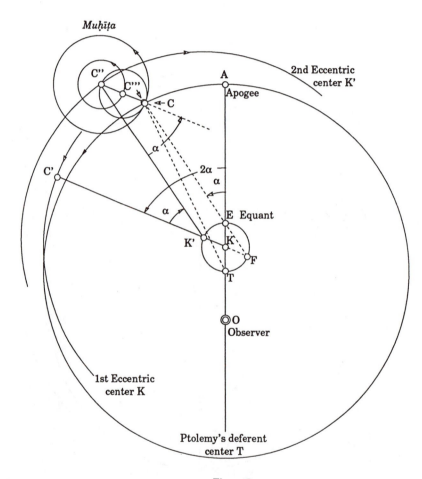

Muḥīṭa

C''

C'''

C

2nd Eccentric
center K'

A
Apogee

α

2α
α

C'

α

E Equant

α

K'   K

F

T

O
Observer

1st Eccentric
center K

Ptolemy's deferent
center T

Figure 9
Khafrī's model for the upper planets. In order to bring point C''' to coincide with
point C, he uses two eccentrics with centers K and K' respectively, and either one
epicyclet, borrowed from 'Urḍī and called *al-Muḥīṭa* by Quṭb al-Dīn al-Shīrāzī and
Khafrī and doubled in size, or two redundant 'Urḍī epicyclets, whose diameters are
in line with one another, and only the first one is allowed to move. By completing
the trianlge EKF, one can prove that point C''' will coincide exactly with point C,
thus duplicating the Ptolemaic model.

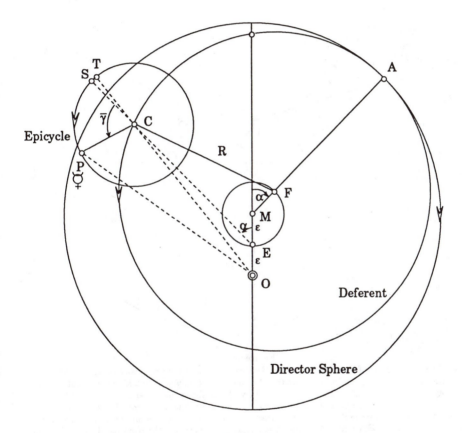

Figure 10
Ptolemy's model for the planet Mercury

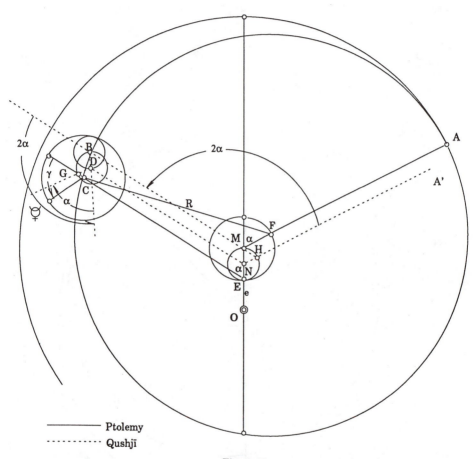

Figure 11

Qushjī's modification of Ptolemy's model for Mercury. By taking a director, with center N, whose eccentricity is equal to one and a half times the Ptolemaic eccentricity, and by taking a deferent whose eccentricity is equal to one half the Ptolemaic eccentricity, Qushjī allows the center of his deferent H to move around a small circle with center N. He then allows the deferent itself to move around its own center H, in the opposite direction, at twice the speed of the director, namely 2α. At the circumference of his deferent he places a small epicyclet, with center B, radius e/2 = NH, and lets it move at the same speed as the deferent, and in the same direction. Now by using 'Urḍi's Lemma he determines that line DN will always be parallel to line BH, because BD=NH, and angle MHN = MBD = 180°- 2α. Therefore point D will look as if it is moving uniformly around point N. By placing another identical epicyclet around point D, and letting it move at half the speed of the first and in the opposite direction, point G, at the circumference of the second epicyclet would then be brought very close to the Ptolemaic center of the epicycle C. In fact the difference between the two points is intentionally exaggerated here for purposes of clarity. By using 'Urḍi's Lemma once more, line GE can be proven to be always parallel to line DN (angle END = NDG = 180°- α, and line GD = EN), thus making point G look as if it is moving uniformly around point E, the required Ptolemaic *Equant*.

The Cartographic Background
to the Voyages of Columbus

David Buisseret

At the back of their minds, Columbus and his contemporaries must have had the earliest and simplest world-image produced by the Europeans. This is the so-called T-O map, shown at its most elementary in plate 1. It is oriented eastwards, and shows the three continents, Asia, Europe and Africa, with the names of the appropriate sons of Adam — Shem, Cham and Jefeth. The continents are separated by the "Great Sea or Mediterranean," while outside them runs the "Ocean Sea."

Columbus was eventually known as the "Admiral of the Ocean Sea," and it is interesting to speculate how he and his contemporaries viewed the T-O maps. While we might be inclined to visualize them as representing a disc, perhaps they should be seen as one half of a sphere, showing the "known land," at the back of which lay the other half of the world, "not yet discovered" as the legends sometimes read.

Whereas T-O maps like this were simply schematic, setting out the basic elements of the world, there were other *mappaemundi* which offered much more detail. A good example of these is the so-called "Beatus" map, which is found in various manuscript versions of Beatus's *Commentary on the Apocalypse.* Plate 2 shows the copy drawn for Gregory, abbot of Saint-Sever in Aquitaine, about 1050. It is oriented to the east, where Adam and Eve may be seen in Paradise. The Mediterrean Sea with its various islands runs up the middle of the map, and then branches leftwards into the Black Sea. To the right, it is balanced by the Red Sea and Persian Gulf. Europe lies to the left, with its provinces named and Britain shown schematically on the outer edge. On the upper right, the map goes as far as India, and the golden oval seems to indicate the island of Sri Lanka (Ceylon).

A map like this contains an immense amount of information, even if it is presented in a way that we do not instantly recognize. Columbus would have seen such maps, often in churches, and would have been familiar with their contents. He also would have been familiar with a different kind of map, that began to emerge in the Mediterranean Sea about 1300. This was the "portolan chart," whose emergence seems to be linked with the adoption of the compass by Mediterranean sailors during the later thirteenth century. The salient characteristics of these charts did not change much for three centuries, and plate 3 shows us a good example of the type from 1456.

The Portolan Chart of the Mediterranean area was drawn by Petrus Roselli on animal skin with the neck to the left. The outline of the Mediterranean coasts is shown with great fidelity, and the place-names along the coast are written at right-angles to it. Some great cities, like Venice, Cologne, and Avignon, are shown by sketches, and flags indicate the lands of the different rulers. Some scale-bars are inserted, but there is no attempt to provide figures of latitude or longitude. Roselli had some knowledge of the British Isles, but his information petered out roughly where the coast of Belgium now is. His knowledge of the west coast of Africa was also quite limited, but he inserts a fair number of Atlantic islands.

During the fifteenth century, maps of this kind were used to plot not only the west coast of Africa, as the Portuguese slowly worked their way southwards along it, but also an increasing number of Atlantic islands. Plate 4 shows one of the most famous of these maps. It was drawn by Zuane Pizzigano in 1424, and shows the coasts of Europe and Africa much as they would be shown by Roselli: its great novelty consists in the large islands shown out in the Atlantic. The plotting of these islands, one of which was named "Antilia," reminds us that there were many rumors of land to the west during the fifteenth century. Columbus would have been well aware both of these rumors and of maps like the one produced by Pizzigano.

He also would have known about the corpus of maps associated with the name of Claudius Ptolemy, who lived in the second century A.D. in Alexandria, and whose "Geography" provides a summary of ancient knowledge of the globe, in the shape of a long series of figures of latitude and longitude for many places in the world known in his time. From these figures a series of maps was derived, though not, it would appear, by Ptolemy himself. The first manuscript versions of the "Geography" began to circulate in western Europe in the early fifteenth century; it was first printed in 1477 and thereafter went into many editions. Columbus owned a copy of the edition of 1479.

Plate 5 shows the world map from a manuscript of the "Geography," edited in Florence in 1474 by Donnus Nicolaus Germanus, and now preserved in the Vatican Library. This map offers a remarkable summary of the strengths and weaknesses of antique cartography. Astonishingly, the British Isles and even Scandinavia are well portrayed, as is the Mediterranean region. *Terra incognita* rings the southern edge of the known world, well to the south of the equator. The Indian subcontinent is summarily indicated, with an immense Sri Lanka (Taprobana) out in the Indian Ocean; perhaps this is a misreading of some larger island like Sumatra. In the east, solid land appears to link up with the southern continent.

What sharply distinguishes this map from its predecessors is the presence of a scale of latitude and longitude around its edges. Beginning at zero on the equator, the scale runs north to latitude 65 (top right on the map); the longitude runs from zero off the Spanish Coast, eastwards to 180 degrees at the point where Asia seems to end. The Ptolemaic invention of a mathematical system for indicating the location of any place on earth was crucial to voyages like that meditated by Columbus, even if, as we shall see, he did not in fact base his calculations upon a correct set of figures.

In addition to the evidence provided by these various kinds of maps, Columbus relied on geographical information derived from a variety of other sources. Indeed, thanks to the survival of six of his books in the Biblioteca Colombina in Seville, we are almost unimaginably well informed about his geographical concepts before and during his four great voyages. The books are:

    (a) a copy of Plutarch's *Lives*,

    (b) a copy of the 1479 edition of Ptolemy's *Geography*,

    (c) an Italian translation, published in 1489, of Pliny's *Natural History*,

    (d) 1485 Latin translation of *Book of Ser Marco Polo*,

    (e) Pierre d'Ailly's *Imago mundi*, published at Louvain in 1483,

    (f) Aeneas Sylvius' *Historia rerum ubique gestarum*, published in 1477.

The latter three books have the additional advantage that they were heavily annotated by Columbus and his brother, thus giving us a very good idea of what ideas they found important or useful.

From Marco Polo (1254-1323), who lived for seventeen years at the court of the Great Khan, Columbus would have learned in particular about the great extent of Asia, which he thought carried it very far to the east and consequently brought it close up against Europe. He also read here about the island of Japan, or Cipangu, which lay in the ocean off the east coast of Asia; for some time he thought that Cuba must be this Cipangu.

Pierre d'Ailly, Cardinal of Cambrai, composed his *Imago mundi* about 1410. It contained the message about the great extent of Asia; as d'Ailly put it, "the beginnings of the Orient and of the Occident are close." Much the same information could be found in the *Historia* of Aeneas Sylvius, whose work was largely a conflation of the ideas of Ptolemy and of Marco Polo. Sylvius emphasized the peaceable nature of the people of China, whereupon Columbus noted "and this at the beginning of India, right opposite Spain and Ireland." It was a curious coincidence that when Columbus landed after his first voyage, he found himself among the Arawaks, who were perhaps the most peaceable peoples of the whole eastern littoral of the Americas; no wonder he thought that he was in China! From Sylvius, too, he derived information about groups who were cannibals and others who were Amazons; these ideas would color his reaction to the peoples he encountered.

In Pliny, finally, Columbus would find confirmation of his idea that Morocco and "India," were close. Or as Aristotle was said to have remarked, "between the end of Spain and the beginning of India is a small sea navigable in a few days." Among the medieval texts, then, Columbus found ample encouragement for his idea that he would strike Asia quite soon after sailing west from Spain. In the years immediately preceding his first voyage, this concept began to appear on maps and globes.

It is best exemplified in the work of Henricus Martellus Germanus, who probably came from Nürnberg, and worked at Florence in the 1480s and 1490s. Four copies survive of his small manuscript world map, and one of a large (6 feet by 4 feet) manuscript world wall map, now preserved at the Beinecke Library at Yale University (Plate 6). This map, which has partially deteriorated, is of extraordinary importance because, unlike the smaller copies, it includes figures both of latitude and of longitude, and so leads us into an understanding of what Columbus believed before he sailed in 1492. He may even have seen a printed copy of this map; it certainly conformed to his views.

The figures of latitude run from 40 degrees south to 85 degrees north, taking in the north coast of Russia and, to the south, a much improved version of Africa, following the voyage by Bartholomew Diaz in 1488. The figures of longitude run from 5 degrees west, somewhere near the Madeira islands, all the way to 270 degrees east, off the coast of Asia. Here we see a crucial extension to the image offered by the small maps, for Germanus now includes off Asia an island-studded sea and also a representation of the island of Cipangu, or Japan.

If this part of the world really comprised 270 degrees, or three-quarters of the whole, then only 90 degrees could remain to be traversed between Cipangu and Spain (the true figure is something like 200 degrees). To this gross underestimate Columbus then added other "Corrections," all in the sense of underestimating the distance, until in the end he calculated that he had about 2400 nautical miles to sail from the Canaries to Cipangu. The true figure is something over 10,000 nautical miles, which was not a distance that Columbus could have contemplated; the enterprise would have been dead before it began.

The cartographic ideas of Martellus were quite widely held by about 1490, and may indeed have inspired the first surviving world globe. It was constructed by Martin Behaim of Nürnberg, where it is still preserved in the German National Museum. Behaim had extensive contacts in Portugal, and was acquainted with the latest cartographic ideas. His globe is richly inscribed, and has many legends describing the various countries; off the Cape of Good Hope, for instance, we read that "[i]t is summer in this country when we have winter, and when we have winter, it is summer for them." Flags fly above the territories of the various European sovereigns, and drawings mark prominent towns. Plate 7 shows the northern quarter of this globe from Cipangu on the left to the coast of Europe and Africa on the right.

In Behaim's concept of the world, the distance from the Azores to the outlying islands of Asia was roughly fifty degrees of latitude, less than he believed the length of the Mediterranean Sea to be. He calculated the distance from the Canaries to Cipangu as three thousand eighty nautical miles, almost seven hundred miles more than Columbus, but still a possible distance, particularly if mariners could find shelter in some of the numerous islands that dotted his ocean, as they also filled the sea off the east Asian coast of Martellus.

The work of Martellus and Behaim seems to summarize the way in which Columbus must have visualized the world just before his first voyage. However, both Christopher Columbus and his brother Bartholomew are known to have made charts, and it is possible that a chart now preserved at the Bibliothèque Nationale in Paris was actually drawn by, or perhaps for them, about 1492. This chart, reproduced as plate 8, consists of two parts. On the right is a conventional map, in the portolan chart style, of western Europe and northwestern Africa. Its nomenclature is largely Portuguese, and it takes in recent Portuguese explorations on the African coast. On the left-hand side of the chart is a circular *mappamundi*, showing the world with Jerusalem at its center; this map has a well developed treatment of the east coast of southern Africa, which has led some commentators to ascribe it to some date after Vasco da Gama's visit to those parts in 1499.

In 1924, the French historian Charles de la Roncière put forward the argument that this chart was probably the work of Columbus. He founded this assertion on the contents of some of the inscriptions; two hundred eleven of them conform to what we know of Columbus's experience, a reference at the Cape Verde islands mentions that they were discovered by the Genoese, and in the inscription that flanks the Red Sea, a quotation from the *Imago mundi*, there is an error that also appears in Columbus's marginal notes to that work

More recently, it has been observed that in a note in his copy of the *Imago mundi* Columbus refers the reader to his "four charts on paper, all of which also contain a sphere." As such charts are extraordinarily unusual, this is perhaps the most telling evidence suggesting that Columbus was the author of this chart. However, even if this be granted, the chart does not tell us much more than we already know about his geographical ideas, since it does not bear on the problem of the distance between Asia and Europe. What it may tell us is that Columbus either was an accomplished mapmaker himself, or that he had access to persons with such skills.

Once the first journey had been accomplished, the new-found lands had to recorded. Nothing seems to survive from the last years of the fifteenth century, but from the year 1500 we have the remarkable world-map of Juan de La Cosa, now preserved at the Museo Naval in Madrid (Plate 9). This map, measuring roughly three feet by six feet, was probably the work of a pilot and cosmographer who accompanied Columbus on his first and second voyages. It tellingly reveals the strengths and weaknesses of European cartography at the beginning of the sixteenth century.

On the right-hand side of the map, Europe, Africa and Asia are delineated in the customary portolan-chart style. The outline of Africa is now much better known, but there is still no attempt to relate this known area to the earth as a whole, by inserting figures of latitude and longitude. The lands across the Ocean Sea are thus shown almost in a separate map on the left-hand side. The Greater Antilles are shown convincingly and in roughly the right place, but they are far out of scale with the right-hand side of the map.

To the west of the area explored by Columbus lay *terra incognita*, here covered over by the image of Saint Christopher bearing the Christ-child. To the south lies a coastline that was beginning to be explored, but which is shown as projecting grotesquely far towards Africa. To the north is the "sea discovered by the English," fringed by an immense landmass that also extends much too far back towards Europe. Perhaps, indeed, the green areas on the left-hand side of this great chart are not intended to represent landmasses, but are merely decorative.

Be that as it may, the cartographic equipment carried by Columbus and his contemporaries, largely developed in the restricted latitudes of the Mediterranean Sea, was now faced by a challenge for which it had no answer. There was a need for a global projection for mariners, particularly to take into account the shape of the earth towards the two poles. After many experiments the answer was found in the projection developed by Gerard Mercator, and exemplified in his world map of 1569.

Bibliography

Bagrow, Leo. *History of Cartography*. New edition. Chicago 1985.

Davies, Arthur. "Behaim, Martellus and Columbus." *The Geographical Journal* 143 (1977), 451-59.

Destombes, Marcel. *Mappemondes A.D. 1200-1500*. Amsterdam 1964.

Fernandez-Armato, Felipe. *Columbus and the Conquest of the Impossible*. New York 1974.

Fite, Emerson D., and Archibald Freeman. *A Book of Old Maps*. Cambridge 1926.

Kish, George. *La Carte: Image des civilisations*. Paris 1980.

La Roncière, Charles de. *La carte de Christophe Colomb*. Paris 1924.

Mollat du Jourdin, Michel, and Monique de La Roncière. *Sea Charts of the Early Explorers*. London 1984.

Morison, Samuel Eliot. *Admiral of the Ocean Sea*. 2 vols. Boston 1942.

Nebenzahl, Kenneth. *Atlas of Columbus and the Great Discoveries*. Chicago 1990.

Nunn, George E. *The Geographical Conceptions of Columbus*. New York 1924.

Parry, J.H. *The Age of Reconnaissance*. New York 1983.

Wagner, Henry. "Marco Polo's Narrative becomes Propaganda to inspire Colon." *Imago Mundi* 6 (1950), 3-13.

List of Plates

(1) T-O map from Isidore of Seville's *Etymologiae* (Augsburg, 1472).

(2) World map from Beatus, "Commentaire" (eleventh century). Paris, Bibliothèque Nationale.

(3) Portolan chart of the Mediterranean area by Petrus Roselli, 1456. Chicago, The Newberry Library.

(4) Nautical chart by Zuane Pizzigano, 1424. Minneapolis, The James Ford Bell Library.

(5) World map derived from Claudius Ptolemy, 1474. Rome, The Vatican Library.

(6) World map by Henricus Martellus Germanus, c. 1489. The Beinecke Library, Yale University.

(7) Section from a copy of the Behaim Globe, 1492. Paris, Bibliothèque Nationale.

(8) Chart attributed to Christopher Columbus, c. 1492. Paris, Bibliothèque Nationale.

(9) Detail from the world map by Juan de La Cosa, 1500. Madrid, Museo Naval.

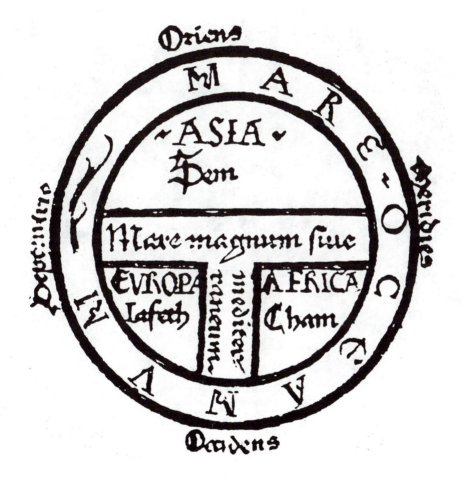

1 T-O map from Isidore of Seville's *Etymologiae* (Augsburg 1472).

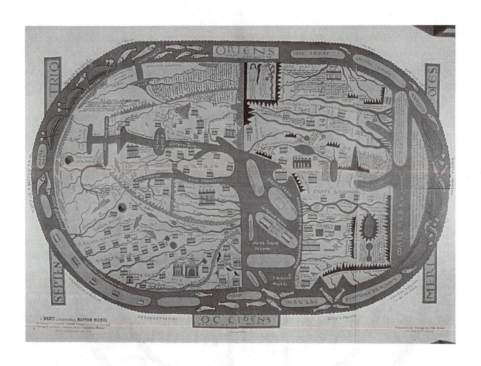

2 World map from Beatus, "Commentaire" (eleventh century). Paris, Bibliothèque Nationale.

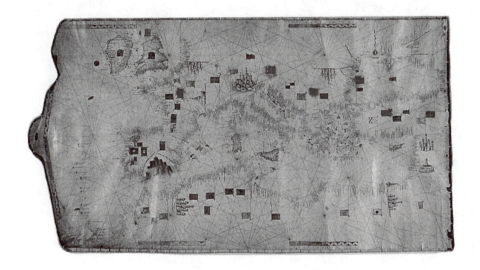

3 Portolan chart of the Mediterranean area by Petrus Roselli, 1456.
Chicago, The Newberry Library.

4 Nautical chart by Zuane Pizzigano, 1424. Minneapolis, The James
Ford Bell Library.

5 World map derived from Claudius Ptolemy, 1474. Rome, The Vatican Library.

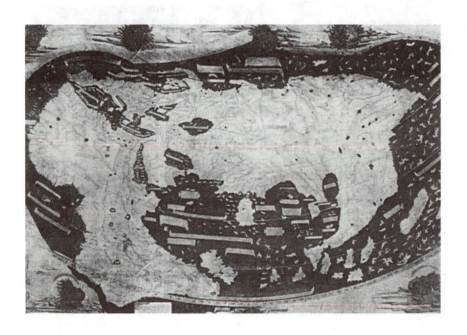

6 World map by Henricus Martellus Germanus, c. 1489. The Beinecke Library, Yale University.

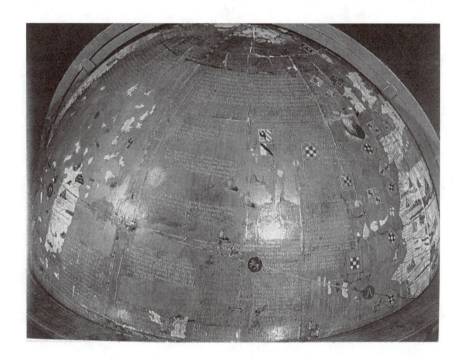

7 Section from a copy of the Behaim Globe, 1492. Paris, Bibliothèque Nationale.

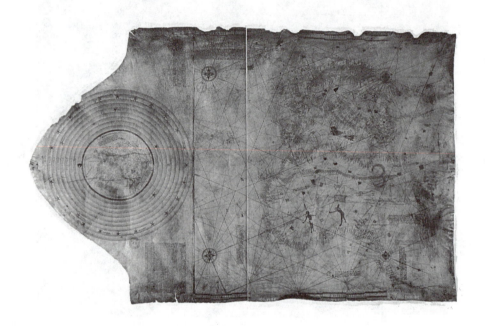

8 Chart attributed to Christopher Columbus, c. 1492. Paris, Bibliothèque Nationale.

9 World map by Juan de La Cosa, 1500. Madrid, Museo Naval.

III
The Voyage

The Imagined World
of Christopher Columbus

Delno C. West

Explorers rarely go forth and probe about. [1] Especially important to explorers of all ages is the role of imagination in geography. Preconceived notions inspired them to envision the unknown environment of *terrae incognitae* before they sailed causing them to search for definite objects which they believed to exist based on the information they had. Such information can be empirical or nonempirical. [2] Thus, to Columbus, and others like him in the fifteenth century, the Ocean space was a mental problem to be solved, to be imagined, before he sailed in order to cross it successfully. In 1492 Christopher Columbus had a geographic image of the other side of the world which was held by many; but that image changed for him; and very quickly (within fifty years) for educated Europeans that image came to manifest a better reality of the globe of the earth.

Crossing the Ocean Sea in 1492 was first and foremost an intellectual problem causing Columbus to become a voracious reader. He studied, cited, or referenced over sixty ancient, medieval, and contemporary authors from three cultures: Jewish, Moslem and Christian to arrive at a mental picture of the ocean space before he left on the first voyage. The majority of these texts he read dealt with geography, cosmology, and related sciences such as meteorology and natural science, or with the Holy Bible and bible commentaries. [3] Since the Holy Bible (including extra-canonical texts) was the foundation, or source, of most knowledge in the fifteenth century, the Scriptures were just as important to the mind of Columbus as scientific treatises. Indeed, the Scriptures offer a great deal of geographic information to the careful student. Thus, Columbus based his thinking on fifteen hundred years of scientific knowledge and had a well-formed and well-thought-out image of the world when he sailed in 1492.

Ancient and medieval writers whom Columbus studied had different ideas about the size of the earth and the ratio of land surfaces to oceans. In the fifteenth century, there was never any debate over the shape of the earth since educated men had known it to be a sphere since ancient times. In the European Renaissance, cosmological and geographical arguments centered on the circumference of the globe, the length of a degree, the size of the *Oecumene* (i.e. landmass of Africa, Europe and Asia), the disposition on the globe of land and water, whether the equator could be crossed to reach all the areas of the world, the advisability of "sailing under the earth" (i.e. to the other side) because it might he impossible to return, debates over distances, wind and current patterns, the logistics of long ocean voyages, and the possibility of a fourth landmass which would make the earth symmetrical. These were the issues with which Columbus had to deal in order to "sell" his plan to learned commissions appointed by the governments he approached. Perhaps the most important question he had to resolve to everyone's satisfaction was whether science and technology in the fifteenth century was capable of making such a journey into unknown space.

We can see, primarily through map traditions, that Columbus's configuration of the world (i.e. a single elongated landmass surrounded by the Ocean Sea) was essentially a medieval tradition while his cartography was state-of-the-art Renaissance knowledge. Even though Columbus made a living, with his brother, drawing maps (presumably portolan sea charts) no map indisputably drawn by him exists, and there is only one map we can be sure he saw during his lifetime. But we do know that Columbus had four kinds of maps available to him: (1) medieval *mappaemundi* and Macrobian maps, (2) Renaissance maps based on ancient authorities such as Ptolemy, (3) portolan sea charts, and (4) literary and mythical descriptions of places which might or might not exist. The combined information from such a diversity of sources produced a European "world view" in the fifteenth century that was a mixture of reality, scientific theory, exotic tales, and mythology. [4]

There are, of course, many sources for Columbus's ideas, but here maps have been chosen to demonstrate Columbus's views because maps are a graphic way to portray how world views were defined. Maps were, and still are, powerful tools for making statements about the world and about ourselves. A map maker, or his sponsor, uses this device to convince you to see things his way. Map makers are highly selective in their representations of reality. They show a point of view and reflect both the knowledge and attitude of the culture from which they come.

Let us begin, then, by looking at medieval *mappaemundi* as one source which shaped Columbus's image of the other side of the world. The term *mappaemundi* literally means "cloth of the world" as these maps tended to be drawn on that medium. A *mappaemundi* is a world diagram, but it includes much more than geographic information. It also encompassed zoological, anthropological, moral, theological and historical information. These maps were normally placed in churches to enable the Christian viewer to place biblical information into the context of time and space.

Mappaemundi evolved from the so-called T-O maps of the ancient world. Using Roman models, Isidore of Seville set the medieval standard as seen in plate 1. In a T-O map, the singular landmass of the world is divided into three parts and surrounded by the Ocean Sea. The landmass is split on a north-south axis by the Mediterranean Sea, while the Don and Nile rivers separate the continents horizontally. But with Isidore, the map has already become a religious statement as he places the east to the top, thus allowing Jerusalem to become the center of the world, and he assigns the three continents to the sons of Noah — Shem, Ham and Jepheth. [5] Plate 2 demonstrates the same concept, but now the landmass is drawn out.

In time, the T-O map became very elaborate as can he seen in the so-called "Cotton Map" from the tenth century, or the so-called "Psalter Map" from the thirteenth century, or the famous Hereford map from the Hereford Cathedral in England. [6] For our purposes, however, the Ebstorf Map (plate 3) serves as an excellent example. The Ebstorf Map was drawn around A.D. 1235 and was held by the Benedictine monastery at Ebstorf until destroyed by allied bombers during World War II. It was a very large map, as are most of these elaborate *mappaemundi*, nearly twelve feet by twelve feet in size.

The Ebstorf Map is still a T-O pattern, but now superimposed over the body of Christ who holds the world in his arms. Jerusalem is at the center (navel) with Christ's head near the Garden of Eden and his feet protruding out through the Straits of Gibraltar. The map locates almost every important Christian site, both real and imagined. As with nearly all these maps, the Garden of Eden was believed to be a real place and located on the edge of Asia. [7] The wall encircling part of Asia is both the great wall of China (about which Europeans had heard), and more importantly, the wall built by Alexander the Great to fence in the forces of Gog and Magog. Off the coast of Asia are islands which are labeled as islands of gold and silver. Although such a map could show the pilgrim the general way to Jerusalem and on to Asia, locating biblical sites along the way, its purpose was more to aid the Christian to visualize the geographic setting of biblical stories.

The culmination of the *mappaemundi* tradition is the map drawn by the famous cartographer, Fra Mauro of Venice c. 1459 (plate 4). Commissioned by King Alfonso IV of Portugal, Fra Mauro was influenced by contemporary portolan sea charts, information brought to Europe by Marco Polo, and possibly by Islamic map makers (which would explain why he drew his map with south at the top — a common practice of Moslem cartographers). Although less obvious, the most important Christian sites are still shown (e.g. the Garden of Eden is in the lower corner with a line placing it on the edge of Asia). Off the coast of Asia, Fra Mauro drew a sea full of islands because Marco Polo reported that there were thousands of islands off that coast in the Ocean Sea. Such data was extremely important to Columbus who argued that logistically the trip he proposed was much more feasible as he could always re-supply his ships from these islands if he needed to. Fra Mauro also described some of these islands as lands of gold and silver, again impor-tant information for Columbus and his venture capital investors.

A parallel tradition to the tripartite *mappaemundi* legacy was the quadripartite heritage of Beatus of Libania. This map (plate 5) was drawn to illustrate Beatus's large commentary on the Apocalypse writ-ten in the eighth century. Although the original of this map has not sur-vived, a large number of copies do exist, including two cut into stone at Vezelay and Moissac. Beatus located the Garden of Eden and the islands of gold and silver off the coast of Asia, but he also indicated that there might be an unknown continent of the antipodes separated from the known landmass. In classical thinking, some speculated that the world had to be symmetrical either by a fourth continent below Asia (i.e. Europe-Africa, Asia-unknown), or another single landmass on the opposite side of the world to balance the landmass familiar to ancient geographers.

Another way of visualizing the world in the Middle Ages was the Macrobian model. Macrobius, a fifth-century monk influenced by ancient Greek precedents, divided the world into five climatic zones with an inhabited north divided from the unknown world on the other side of the planet, in this case to the south (plate 6). Beginning with a frigid north, which is balanced by a frigid south, inhabited latitudes stretch to the middle torrid zone which is impassable. Climatic or zonal maps in the Macrobius tradition are the only definitely known maps seen by Columbus as this is the way in which Cardinal Pierre d'Ailly drew the world in his *Imago mundi*. The *Imago mundi* was Columbus's favorite book about the earth and its physical configuration. [8] In his own copy which survives, he left eight hundred ninety-eight marginal notes. D'Ailly's map (plate 7) is a sophisticated variation of the Macro-bian model which includes elements of medieval *mappaemundi*. A case could he made that Columbus was a zonal sailor who rarely left the middle temperate zones.

What did Columbus learn from these traditions? Basically, they caused him to form his vision of what was across the Ocean Sea, on the opposite side of the globe, and what constituted the size, shape and content of the planet Earth. Columbus's imagination was deeply rooted in the cosmology and geography of the Middle Ages. These traditions shaped his exploration agenda and affected the way in which he described the unknown regions of the world he found. On his third voyage, for example, he clearly believed that he had found the site of the Garden of Eden after recognizing the continent of South America. And, on the fourth voyage, as another example, he believed that he had found the lost gold mines (and those gold and silver regions on *mappae-mundi*) of King Solomon of the Old Testament in what is today Panama. [9]

Columbus's practical understanding of the Ocean Sea, however, was more a product of the fifteenth century and relied on new carto-graphic thinking being developed by Renaissance geographers. In their passionate search for ancient texts and authorities, Renaissance scholars began to base their thinking on the theories of the second century astronomer, mathematician and geographer Claudius Ptolemy. His geographic writings were translated and introduced to the West in the fifteenth century to provide a new perspective of the world. But as was the case with many ancient authorities, Ptolemy was not always right. His errors greatly encouraged Columbus.

Plate 8 is a typical Renaissance Ptolemaic map of the world as drawn in Florence, Italy in 1474. A grid is placed over the world to give it more coherence, but it greatly miscalculates the size of the globe by elongating Eurasia. Indeed, Asia stretches clear off the map to some unknown length into the Ocean Sea in the east. In his writings, Ptolemy had estimated Eurasia to stretch some one hundred eighty degrees across the planet (it is actually about 100 degrees). Thus, Ptolemy encouraged Columbus in his miscalculation of the size of the earth and the relative sizes of the Eurasian landmass to the Ocean Sea.

But this was important supporting evidence for Columbus. He relied, in the first instant, on Pierre d'Ailly (*Imago mundi*) who had borrowed his information wholesale from Roger Bacon's *Opus maius*. To make things worse, Columbus went to Il Mina on the coast of Africa thinking he was much closer to the equator than he actually was in order to make his own estimate of the circumference of the globe. Using nautical instruments, he arrived at his own conclusions near to those of d'Ailly and supported by Ptolemy. Columbus had settled on the figure of forty nautical miles per degree in calculating the circumference of the earth. Actually, it is sixty nautical miles. In one stroke of his pen, Columbus reduced the size of the earth by twenty percent, or about fourteen thousand four hundred nautical miles (plate 9). Putting this data together, the miscalculations of Ptolemy, d'Ailly and himself, Columbus concluded that the Ocean Sea was fairly small and that the distance from the Canary Islands to Japan should not be more than about two thousand five hundred miles of open ocean with islands scattered along the way. His thinking was that if the planet was small and Eurasia covered at least one hundred eighty degrees of it (Columbus liked Marinus of Tyre's estimate of two hundred twenty-five degrees even better!), and since the biblical Apocryphal text of II Esdras 6:42 told him that God had made the earth six parts land and one part water, then the distance was reduced to a manageable size. These were the theories which caused him to be turned down by every learned commission he argued before. Better minds in Iberian universities had calculated the circumference of the earth at approximately sixty nautical miles per degree making the voyage across the ocean sea too long to be feasible given the technology of the fifteenth century. Fortunately for Columbus and his colleagues on the first voyage, the Americas lay in his way at about three thousand miles!

Portolan sea charts were another type of map known to Christopher Columbus, but important only to the extent that they defined the near Ocean sea: that is, the ocean out as far as the Azores and north to Iceland and south to mid-Africa. Such maps were used by pilots and ship's captains to navigate in the open ocean relying upon rhumb lines to which a windlass could be set enabling the ship to find port. One such map needs brief mention, however, and that is the so-called "Columbus Chart" (plate 10). The Columbus Chart was drawn sometime in the mid 1490's and its author is controversial. [10] The map is a combination of a medieval *mappaemundi* inset in a cosmological diagram next to a portolan sea chart. We know that Columbus drew at least four such charts (as he tells us he did in a marginal note to d'Ailly's *Imago mundi*), but there is no clear evidence that this is one of those maps.

The image Columbus had of the other side of the world in 1492 is probably close to that displayed on the Martin Behaim globe: an open ocean with little in between Europe and Asia. The Behaim globe (plate 11) is the first known attempt to place a map of the world on a globe and was created in 1492 by drawing a world map on gores and attaching them to a paper mache ball. Behaim was a merchant and commercial agent married to the daughter of the governor of Fayal and Pico in the Azores. There is no evidence that Columbus and Behaim ever met, but many have speculated that they may have. [11] Behaim's globe map is a culmination of the several map traditions available to Columbus and depicts common understanding of the world when he sailed. The Ocean Sea on the Behaim globe separates Europe and Asia and supports Columbus's contention that the distance is rather small. The Canary Islands and Chipangu (Japan) are on the same latitude, a belief held by Columbus who set a straight westward course from the Canaries.

But even with sophisticated speculation, the Ocean Sea was still an unknown environment showing only mythical islands and the thousands of islands mentioned by Polo beyond the Azores. Thus, crossing it presented a psychological barrier and offered no suggestions for navigating it. This is why the letter and map of Paolo Toscanelli were of singular importance to Columbus (plate 12). [12] Toscanelli was a medical doctor, mathematician and cartographer in Florence, Italy, and a leading student of Ptolemaic theories. In 1474 the famous mathematician, Nicholas of Cues, died and the funeral was held at Todi. Toscanelli attended the funeral of his old friend and there met Fernan Martins de Roriz, the Canon of the Lisbon Cathedral who also had come to the funeral. Martins was an advisor to the king of Portugal and in charge of the Portuguese navigation committee sponsoring exploration down the African coast. Portuguese exploration activities had reached a crisis by 1474, because they had sailed far enough south to lose sight of their primary guidance mark, the pole star. Ships could coast down Africa, but the return had to be made far out to sea, out of the sight of land, due to the strong southerly coastal winds. Thus, on the open ocean, the pole star was crucial for navigation.

Discussing these difficulties with Toscanelli, Martins was highly interested in the new geographic theories being discussed at Florence, Italy. He asked the elderly doctor to prepare for him, and consequently for the Portuguese king, an ocean map and explanation of his system of navigation on the open sea. Toscanelli did so and his letter and map were duly sent to Portugal. They were subsequently studied by Columbus who copied the letter by his own hand on the back fly leaves of his personal copy of Enea Silvio Piccolomini, *Historia rerum ubique gestarum*. Columbus tells us that he had seen the map which accompanied the letter. Many believe that he took a copy of the Toscanelli map with him on the first voyage.

The Toscanelli correspondence and map provided a system of measurements in the absence of landmarks. [13] Toscanelli combined Ptolemy's gridding system with perspective geometry in his cartography of the Ocean Sea giving metric coherence to it. With such a grid-map, mariners could sail "grid distances" in any direction and return following the same method. What Toscanelli demonstrated to Martins and hence to Columbus was a new sense of conformity to the unknown Ocean Sea. Gridding the sea gave a psychological boost to the mariner because all locations could be fixed in relation to one another by coordinates, and by extension, unknown sites could be brought into harmony and proportion to the whole. As Samuel Edgerton has pointed out:

> Whatever the configuration of a grid-divided surface, the observer is able to comprehend all of its continuity as long as he can relate to the side of at least one undistorted, modular square which represents the true unit of measurement for judging the whole. [14]

Using such a map, Columbus was able to visualize the Ocean Sea as a sea-link between continents and to conceptualize the earth under a series of grids. Writing to Pope Alexander VI about his first voyage, Columbus expressed himself in such terms by telling the pontiff: "I had gone ten lines into the other hemisphere." [15]

Columbus made four voyages and each changed his view somewhat about the configuration of the world. On the first and second voyages he sailed among the various Caribbean islands. On the third voyage he found South America coasting its northwest shoreline. On the fourth voyage he sailed up and down the meso-american coastline of Central America.

Two maps give us some indication of how Columbus viewed the other side of the world and the Ocean Sea after the four voyages. The maps are the famous Piri Re'is Chart of the Ocean Sea (plate 13) and the free-hand drawing done by Bartholomew Colón, Christopher's brother, for Pope Alexander VI (plate 14).

In 1501 a naval battle was fought between Turkish and Spanish vessels during which a Spanish sailor was captured by the Turkish admiral Kemal Re'is. The sailor had made three trips across the Ocean Sea with Christopher Columbus and had a packet of charts, at least one of which was drawn by the famous admiral, in his possession. Piri Re'is, nephew of Kemal Re'is, had sailed with his uncle for many years and had become an experienced cartographer by constantly keeping notes and drawings of harbors, compass bearings, reefs, hidden rocks and the like. When Kemal Re'is died in 1511, Piri Re'is spent the next two years at Gallipoli drawing a world map. It is probable that his project was supported by the sultan, and certainly it was known about in official circles. Piri Re'is tells us that he used twenty some maps from a variety of sources, both east and west, to construct his map clearly stating that he used the map captured by his uncle and drawn by the Genoese, "Colombo," for the Ocean Sea. Only the western half of the Re'is map survives. Plate 13 is the result of that endeavor.

Plate 14, on the other hand, is a sketch map drawn by Bartholomew Colón sometime between 1503-1506. After the fourth voyage, Columbus sent his brother to Rome to petition Pope Alexander VI to pressure King Ferdinand to colonize and christianize the lands he had found. Before his audience with the pope, however, Bartholmew talked with Alexander Zorzi, a Venetian who collected exploration stories. Zorzi convinced Bartholomew to embellish Columbus's letter with a map of the discoveries. Bartholomew, who was close to his brother throughout the New World adventure, undoubtedly held the same views as his famous brother. His map shows Columbus's discoveries to be on the edge of Asia. The Caribbean Islands stand between Europe and Asia and the South American continent is attached to the Eurasian land mass. Comparing this map to the globe of Martin Behaim shows some change in Columbus's imagination, but not much. Most notable is the addition of *Novo Mundo* jutting southeast from the coast of the Asian mainland.

Knowledge about the other side of the world spread rapidly. The oldest extant map depicting Columbus's discoveries is one drawn by Juan de la Cosa in 1500 (plate 15). De la Cosa accompanied Columbus on his first voyage, and he made three other trips to the New World with Ojeda and Vespucci. The map reflects Renaissance cartography, but with elements of medieval symbolism. Europe, for example, is dim and drab while the new territories to the West are lush and green. Columbus is pictured as St. Christopher carrying the Christ child to the new lands. The rose compass positioned in the ocean shows the Holy family perhaps blessing the new discoveries. On the other hand, the coast lines are becoming accurate and South America and the Caribbean reflect Juan de la Cosa's experience sailing in those regions. This is also the earliest map to contain both the discoveries of Columbus and John Cabot. North America has taken shape and place names are visible along the far northern coasts. Scholars have assumed that de la Cosa had access to the lost charts of Cabot. It is unclear, however, whether de la Cosa thought these new lands a part of Asia or separate mainlands.

In 1507, Martin Waldseemüller drew his famous map in Strassburg (plate 16). His consultant was another noted early explorer and friend of Columbus, Amerigo Vespucci. Waldseemüller based his map on Ptolemaic principles revised by influences from Marco Polo's *Il Milione*, but the important addition is information gained from early explorers. He shows the New World totally separate from Asia with a sea in between. He, of course, honored his consultant by naming the new southern continent "America."

By 1544, shortly after Coronado entered what would become the southwestern United States, and only fifty-two years after Columbus's first voyage, Sebastian Cabot published his world map at Antwerp. The son of John Cabot who sailed from England to North America in 1497, Sebastian became the Pilot Major of Spain during the reign of Charles V. An explorer himself who made trips to the New World, Sebastian Cabot's state-of-the-art map was an instant "best seller" throughout Europe bringing current geographic knowledge to the educated public (plate 17). The map is anthropological and zoological as well as geographical. South America is well defined as is the east coast of North America. The southwest part of North America is defined up to today's California. Clearly, Cabot, and other scientists by the mid-sixteenth century, knew that North and South America were separate continents, and that there was a large ocean between them and Asia. The other side of the world no longer had to be imagined — it was becoming reality!

Notes

[1] Originally this lecture included over fifty map examples. In the interest of economy, only a few of those map traditions are included in this article.

[2] J. Wright, *Human Nature and Geography* (Cambridge 1966), 266. Non-empirical information included a large corpus of myth and legend from the Bible, rumors of ancient and medieval voyages, and word-of-mouth travelers' tales. A study of many of these myths, legends and rumors can be found in M. Campbell, *The Witness of the Other World: Exotic European Travel Writing, 400-1600* (Ithaca 1988). See also, S. Greenblatt, *Marvelous Possessions: The Wonders of the New World* (Chicago 1991).

[3] For a list of works cited by Columbus, see D. West and A. Kling, *The Libro de las profecías of Christopher Columbus* (Gainesville, FL 1991), 22-26. The most modern edition of Columbus's own writings are C. Varela, *Christóbal Colón: Textos y documentos completos* (Madrid 1984), especially the long introduction on how the texts he read influenced his own writings; and V. Flint, *The Imaginative Landscape of Christopher Columbus* (Princeton 1992), 42ff.

[4] There are a number of excellent sources for the history of geography; suggested here are: K. Nebenzahl, *Atlas of Columbus and the Great Discoveries* (New York 1990); Charles Beazely, *The Dawn of Modern Geography* (London 1897); and the recent remarkable work by J.B. Harley and D. Woodward, *The History of Cartography* (Chicago 1987), I.

[5] In the Old Testament, the sons of Noah go forth to repopulate the earth (Gen. 9:19).

[6] The Cotton Map can be found in the British Library, *Cotton Tiberius* B.V., f. 56ᵛ; the Psalter Map in the British Library, Add. 28681, f. 9; and the Hereford Map still hangs in the Hereford Cathedral. These maps have been reproduced in various studies about historical geography.

[7] A.-D. von den Brincken, "Mappa mundi und Chronographla: Studien zur *imago mundi* des abendlandischen Mittelalters," *Deutsches Archiv für Erforshung des Mittelalters* 24 (1969), 167. Also see my article, "Christopher Columbus, Lost Biblical Sites and the Last Crusade," *The Catholic Historical Review* 78 (1992), 519-41.

[8] Flint, 36-37. For d'Ailly's influence on Christopher Columbus see, P. Watts, "Prophecy and Discovery: On the Spiritual Origins of Christopher Columbus's 'Enterprise of the Indies,' " *American Historical Review* 90 (1985), 73-102.

[9] West, "Columbus, Lost Biblical Sites and Last Crusade," 535.

[10] Nebenzahl, 22-25; D. Quinn, "Columbus and the North: England, Iceland, and Ireland," *The William and Mary Quarterly*, 64 (1992), 288-90; and D. West, "Christopher Columbus and His Enterprise to the Indies: Scholarship of the Last Quarter Century," *The William and Mary Quarterly* 64 (1992), 268.

[11] E.G. Ravenstein, *Martin Behaim, His Life and His Globe* (London 1908), 32-33 for arguments for and against this.

[12] The standard study is H. Vignaud, *Toscanelli and Columbus: The Letter and Chart of Toscanelli* (London 1902).

[13] I have relied heavily upon S. Edgerton, "Florentine Interest in Ptolemaic Cartography as Background for Renaissance Painting, Architecture, and the Discovery of America," *Journal for the Society of Architectural Historians* 33 (1974), 275-92.

[14] Ibid., 287.

[15] Letter to Pope Alexander VI, February, 1502 in Verala, 311.

List of Plates

PLATE 1: Isidore of Seville, 7th century, T-O map, from the first printed edition of *Etymologies*, Augsburg, 1472.

PLATE 2: Simon Marmion world map in Jean Mansel, *Fleur des Histoires*, Bibliothèque Royale Albert 1er, Brussels.

PLATE 3: Ebstorf Mappaemundi, 13th century, drawn for Ebstorf Monastery and destroyed in 1943 during an air raid. Kloster Ebstorf.

PLATE 4: Fra Mauro, ca. 1459, World Map, Biblioteca Nazionale Marciana, Venice.

PLATE 5: Beatus of Liebana, 8th century, World Map, from 12th century copy, British Library.

PLATE 6: Macrobius, 5th century, Climatic or Zonal Map, University of Leyden Library.

PLATE 7: Pierre D'Ailly, 1410, Climatic or Zonal Map, from *Imago mundi*, Biblioteca Colombina, Seville.

PLATE 8: Claudius Ptolemy, 2nd century, World Map. A 1474 copy of original, Biblioteca Apostolica Vaticana, Vatican.

PLATE 9: Donald L. Williams, University of Southern Mississippi, 1989.

PLATE 10: So-Called Christopher Columbus Chart, 1590s, Portolan Sea Chart and Mappaemundi, Bibliothèque Nationale, Paris.

PLATE 11: Martin Behaim, 1492, World Globe, Germanisches National Museum, Nüremberg.

PLATE 12: Paolo Toscanelli, c. 1474, Map of Ocean Sea, as reconstructed from Toscanelli's description by Björn Landstrom, *Columbus* (New York 1966), 20-21.

PLATE 13: Piri Re'is, 1513, Map of Ocean Sea, Topkapi Saray Museum, Istanbul.

PLATE 14: Bartolome Colón, after 1503, Map of Ocean Sea, Biblioteca Nazionale Centrale, Florence.

PLATE 15: Juan de la Cosa, 1500, Map of Ocean Sea, Museo Naval, Madrid.

PLATE 16: Martin Waldseemüller, 1507, World Map, Schloss Wolfegg, Württemberg.

PLATE 17: Sebastian Cabot, 1544, World Map, Bibliothèque Natio-nale, Paris.

PLATE 1: Isidore of Seville, 7th century, T-O map, from the first printed edition of *Etymologies*, Augsburg, 1472.

PLATE 2: Simon Marmion world map in Jean Mansel, *Fleur des Histoires*, Bibliothèque Royale Albert 1er, Brussels.

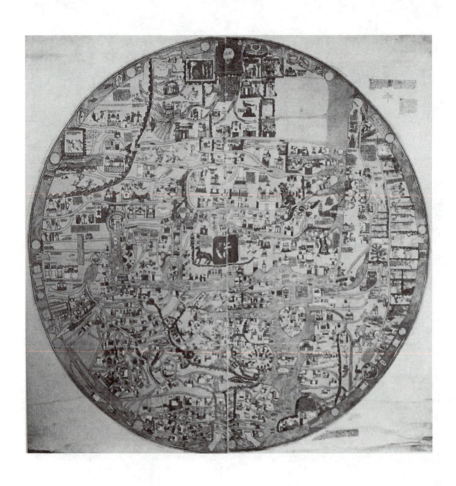

PLATE 3: Ebstorf Mappaemundi, 13th century, drawn for Ebstorf Monastery and destroyed in 1943 during an air raid. Kloster Ebstorf.

PLATE 4: Fra Mauro, ca. 1459, World Map, Biblioteca Nazionale Marciana, Venice.

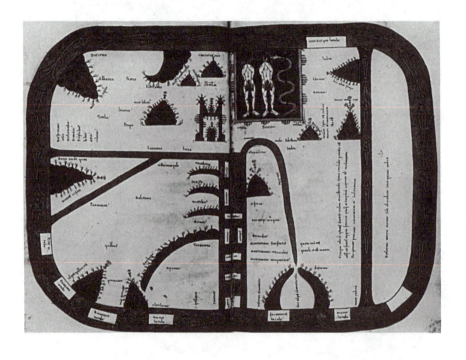

PLATE 5: Beatus of Liebana, 8th century, World Map, from 12th century copy, British Library.

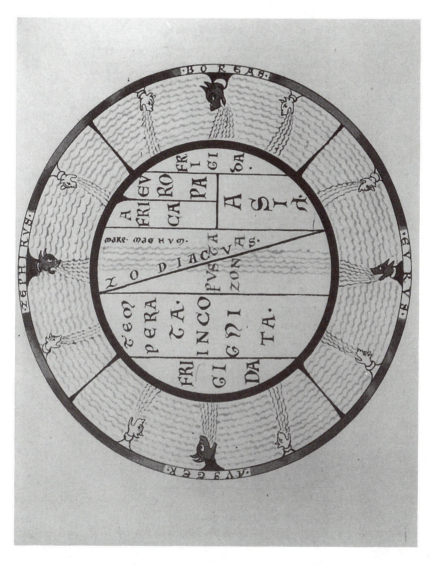

PLATE 6: Macrobius, 5th century, Climatic or Zonal Map, University of Leyden Library.

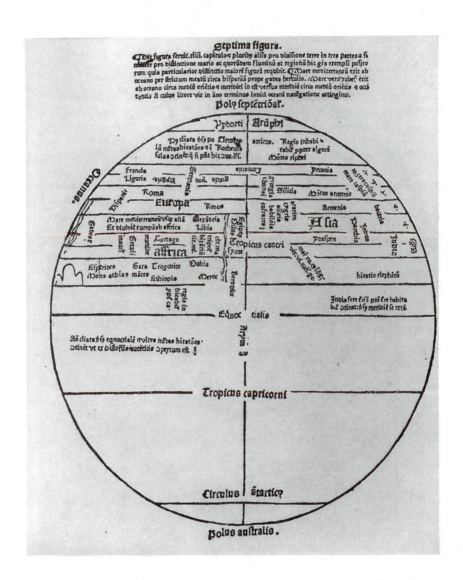

PLATE 7: Pierre D'Ailly, 1410, Climatic or Zonal Map, from *Imago mundi*, Biblioteca Colombina, Seville.

PLATE 8: Claudius Ptolemy, 2nd century, World Map. A 1474 copy of original, Biblioteca Apostolica Vaticana, Vatican.

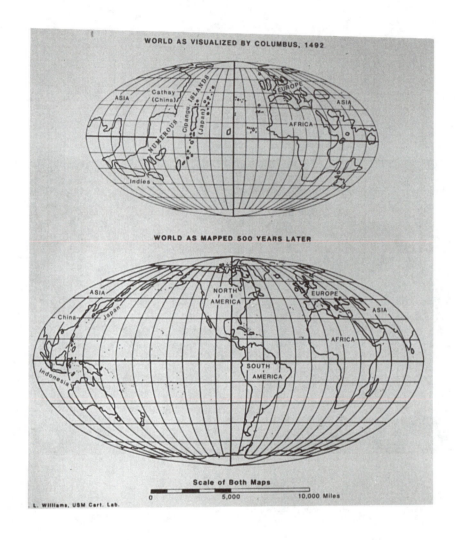

PLATE 9: Donald L. Williams, University of Southern Mississippi, 1989.

PLATE 10: So-Called Christopher Columbus Chart, 1590s, Portolan Sea Chart and Mappaemundi, Bibliothèque Nationale, Paris.

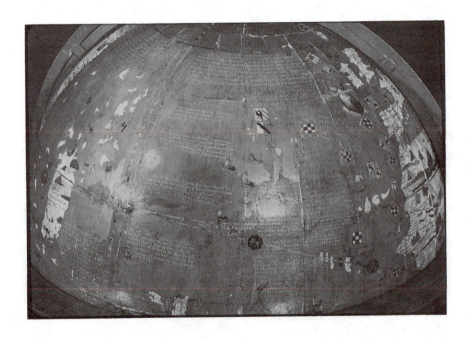

PLATE 11: Martin Behaim, 1492, World Globe, Germanisches National Museum, Nüremberg.

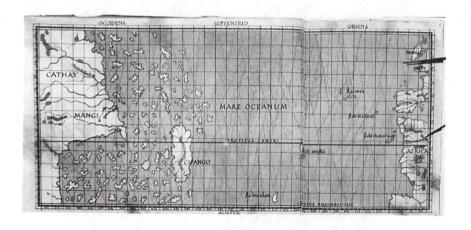

PLATE 12: Paolo Toscanelli, c. 1474, Map of Ocean Sea, as reconstructed from Toscanelli's description by Björn Landstrom, *Columbus* (New York 1966), pp. 20-21.

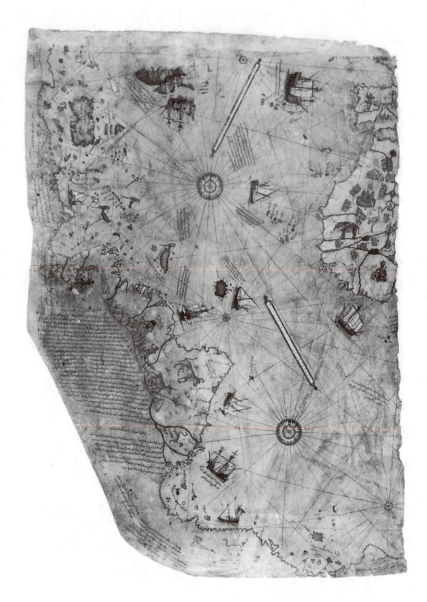

PLATE 13: Piri Re'is, 1513, Map of Ocean Sea, Topkapi Saray Museum, Istanbul.

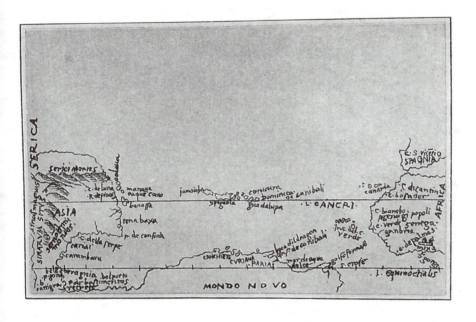

PLATE 14: Bartolome Colón, after 1503, Map of Ocean Sea, Biblioteca Nazionale Centrale, Florence.

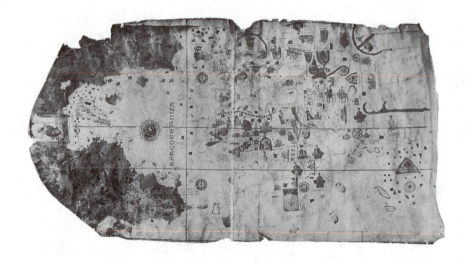

PLATE 15: Juan de la Cosa, 1500, Map of Ocean Sea, Museo Naval, Madrid.

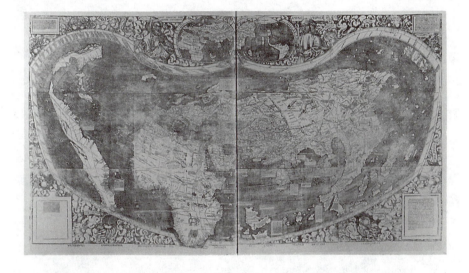

PLATE 16: Martin Waldseemüller, 1507, World Map, Schloss Wolfegg, Württemberg.

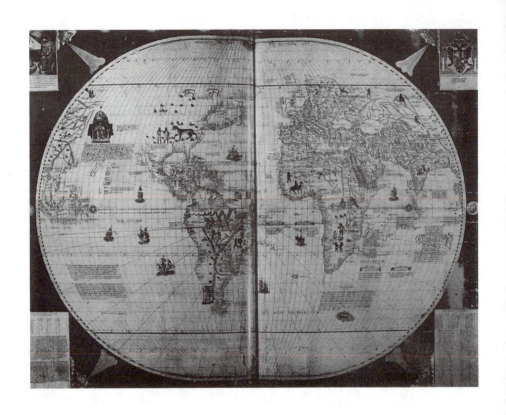

PLATE 17: Sebastian Cabot, 1544, World Map, Bibliothèque
Nationale, Paris.

Columbus's Navigation:

Fifteenth-Century Technology

in Search of Contemporary Understanding

James E. Kelley, Jr.

> "Amaistramente del mar si e per sauer
> ben nauegar." Andrea Bianco, comito di
> galia, Venice, 1436.

Introduction

By 1492, south Europeans had spent three hundred years perfecting a technology for moving men and goods on the high seas. Ship design and operation were coupled with a geometrical navigation using magnetic compass, dividers, and nautical chart. Shipping lanes lay on east-west and north-south strips of the earth's surface — the Mediterranean and Black Seas, and the Atlantic coasts of Europe and Africa. This circumstance made it practical to base charts and navigation calculations on plane geometry.

Columbus's first voyage and the Portuguese penetration of the South Atlantic and Indian Oceans faced Europeans with the general problem of navigating on the sphere. The solution, based on astronomy and spherical trigonometry, was a long time coming. New and old theory and practice came into conflict during the transition, causing mistakes and confusion. The new astronomical navigation dominates writings of the period, giving the impression that the new methods were widely used at an early date. But even among the pioneering Portuguese of 1500 only a handful of pilots could use them.

This study offers alternative perspectives of Columbus's navigation. It underscores inconsistencies between certain traditional views and the historical record. It elaborates the principal navigational processes Columbus used, primarily the "compass and chart" method. The debated issue of the length of Columbus's league is treated in detail, including its connection to contemporary theories of the size of the earth. Also discussed is the early transition to astronomical navigation, the "compass, chart and astrolabe or quadrant" method, and why Columbus probably did not use it. Many details are left to the cited references.

Three conclusions are counter to popular belief or practice: (1) Columbus was a "compass and chart" navigator. His use of a quadrant was experimental, with no definable impact on his navigation during the first voyage. (2) The size of the earth was known only approximately in Europe through the sixteenth century. With possibly one exception, the lengths of contemporary league measures cannot be calculated from the true value of the meridian degree and contemporary equations like "there are 17½ Spanish leagues to the meridian degree." (3) The latitudes of North American places cited in early sixteenth century documents often represent readings from the distorted contemporary maps, not direct measurements with an instrument. This is also true of works by writers with access to the best available data. Caution is needed when using cited latitudes to locate these places.

Overview of the Navigation Processes

Columbus's navigation involved four interrelated processes: [1] pre-voyage planning; ocean navigation; pilotage; and post-voyage analysis. Each process required several repetitive steps of acquiring, observing, recording, manipulating, analyzing, and interpreting data, from which appropriate action was formulated and initiated.

Evidence for much of this model can be found in Bartolomé de las Casas's abstract of the Admiral's *diario de a bordo*, with essential insights and details from other documents. The abstract, called the *Journal*, is a virtually complete record of the voyage, containing navigational details that only a patron who was a working pilot could record. [2] Patrons were required by international maritime law to render an account of the voyage to the shareholders upon its completion. [3] The *diario* and Columbus 's letters fulfilled part of this requirement. This information had many uses. It was essential for planning subsequent voyages. Queen Isabella had a copy made for Columbus's return to the Indies in the fall of 1493. This copy survived through the middle of the sixteenth century when Columbus's grandson, Luis, apparently sold it to finance his debauchery. Fortunately Las Casas made the abstract when planning his *Historia de las Indias*. His manuscript survives in the National Library, Madrid. [4]

Pre-Voyage Planning and Route Strategy

All the expectations and requirements were laid out: initial provisioning, security arrangements, voyage legs and timing, reprovisioning points, and so forth. [5] Insurance rates were based on the plan. The expectations were a gauge of voyage progress, so preemptive action might be taken to blunt potential problems. [6]

Physical conditions along the route were especially important to know. Prevailing or seasonal weather, water conditions (waves, color, temperature), depths and bottoms, birds, fish, whales, weed, islands, obstructions to navigation, and so on, were, to some extent, compiled in contemporary pilot books. Storm frequency tables for various well-travelled areas were also available. [7] The latest intelligence came from mariners newly arrived at port.

Columbus had sailed much of the known Atlantic coastline before his first voyage to America, an expedition planned for years. He knew the fastest way to return home from the Portuguese possessions in west Africa: NNW, out to sea, and north across the trades to the latitude of the Azores to pick up the westerlies for Lisbon. Here were the two wind systems he needed: one to carry him west to the Orient at the latitude of the Canaries, the other east and home at the latitude of the Azores.

Knowledge of political conditions along the route was essential. Prevailing international relations, intelligence from travelers, diplomats, and spies, influenced route selection. [8] Writing of his third voyage, Columbus says "I left ... Wednesday, 30 May [1498] from the town of San Lucar ... and sailed to the island of Madeira by an unusual route, so as to avoid trouble that I might have had with a French armada, that was waiting for me off Cape St. Vincent, and from thence to the Canaries, ..." [9] Columbus assumed the Portuguese would try to intercept him outbound on the first voyage. [10] Three Portuguese caravels sought him when he departed Gomera in early September, 1492. [11] The timing of the fleet's departure on 3 August, which coincided with the departure from Palos of Jewish exiles, was probably one aspect of Columbus's avoidance strategy. [12] With more than the usual numbers of vessels at sea off Cadiz, it would have been difficult to spot him. [13]

Reasonably accurate nautical charts were available for the Mediterranean and Black Seas, and for the coasts of Europe and Africa to well below the equator. [14] Columbus and the pilots required special charts on which to record running position estimates. [15] They would have covered the known world bordering on the Atlantic, from below Cape Verde, north past the Azores, and extending well to the west. [16] All but the eastern margins of the maps would be blank, except for a rhumb net, a mile or league scale, and perhaps indications of the conjectured lands, islands, and other potential hazards to navigation. [17]

Some believe Columbus was guided by a map acquired from Toscanelli, [13] reputed to be similar to a globe of Martin Behaim. [19] Since Martin was in Portugal in 1491, it is presumed he possessed much the same cartographic information as Columbus. Perhaps. Much of this globe is based on Ptolemy, with updating of the Asian parts from the travels of Marco Polo, and very out of date in Columbus's time. [20] Such a map could have speculative value. But Columbus would navigate with a professional chart of greater quantitative validity.

Ocean Navigation

At the core of Columbus's navigation was a formal, disciplined, plane geometrical method for keeping track of the ship's position at sea. It was pioneered by Italians from at least the thirteenth century in conjunction with the magnetic compass and the nautical chart. Through the fifteenth century the method was adopted by all the western sea powers. There are several components of this navigation process.

Holding the Course in Columbus's Time

The helmsman operated the tiller to keep the magnetic compass course bearing aligned with the lubber's line. [21] It took considerable skill. From his position under the stern castle, the helmsman could have seen little, if anything, of the water ahead, or of the activities on deck. He had to have the "feel" of the ship as it pitched and rolled, anticipating and countering each force trying to throw the ship off course. In rough weather two or three other men, or more, might be needed to help. [22] An observer might be stationed nearby to verify the helmsman's constancy. [23] Sail settings were adjusted to assist in maintaining the course.

Columbus's helmsmen had difficulty maintaining the course the first two days out of the Canaries, [24] drawing the Admiral's rebuke. Experienced steering was so important to the accuracy of long distance navigation it was forbidden to permit ship's boys to take the helm. Violation of this rule resulted in the loss of the flagship at Hispaniola on Christmas, 1492.

An Earlier Method of Holding the Course

Prior to the "dry" magnetic compass — a pivoted magnetic needle and compass card, boxed, and mounted in a gimbal [25] — other steering techniques were used. In the twelfth and thirteenth centuries Mediterranean's used "wet" compasses of various designs, in which a lodestone or magnetized needle, floated in a bowl of water, gave a momentary indication of north and south in overcast weather. [26] Using a horizon feature as a temporary bearing mark the helmsman corrected the course. By keeping his wake straight he could proceed for awhile before requiring another course check with the "wet" compass. [27]

The "wet" compass was not practical in turbulent seas. Before about 1300 a.d., the Italian city-states "closed the sea" in winter to reduce shipping risks — typically October through February. With the growing use of the "dry" compass, the helmsman no longer needed to see the horizon or his wake. He and his gear were moved into the tiller room, a relatively dry and wind-free environment under the stern castle. After 1300 a.d., with this improved technology in place, the Italian city-states "closed the sea" only during the most stormy period from about mid-November through mid to late January. [28]

Magnetic Variation and Biased Compasses

By the mid-fifteenth century it was known that the magnetic compass does not point to true north everywhere. The angular difference from true is called magnetic variation. Nurenburg manufacturers of portable sundials began setting the lubber's lines of their magnetic compasses to ½-point east of north. This change improved the accuracy of the dial by making it easy to orient it true in an area of ½-point east variation. Nautical compass makers from Spain to England copied the idea. However, the Genoese continued to install the needle under the north-south rhumb. It was not known that magnetic variation changes from year to year. [29] Consequently, this biased compass type remained in use for over 150 years.

These facts raise interpretive difficulties. Did Columbus sail with Genoese (unbiased) or Sevillian (biased) magnetic compasses on his first voyage? On 16 August 1498, north of the island of Margarita, he noted that some compasses declined more than 1½ points west; others, 2 points west. It seems Columbus had both Genoese and Sevillian compasses on board during the third voyage. On what basis did he use one type or the other? As late as 1615 East India Company ships used a compass offset ½ point east until they crossed the Tropic of Cancer. There they switched to an unbiased compass and measured the variation directly to correct their headings. [30]

Sixteenth-century maps, journals, and sailing directions are probably the key sources for estimating the magnetic variation in the Atlantic in Columbus's time. Several efforts have been made to reconstruct those isogons. The best known is Van Bemmelen's (1899). He assumes, implicitly, that Columbus used a Genoese magnetic compass, and that first landfall was San Salvador. Using his isogons to compute Columbus 's first landfall, as McElroy (1941) and others have done, would seem to involve circular reasoning. [31]

Telling Time Aboard Ship

Fifteenth-century pendulum and gravity clocks would not function properly at sea. Mariners depended on at least three other types of timekeepers, each with a different function, seldom agreeing.

In the northern hemisphere the rotation of the Little Dipper around the celestial pole was used as a nighttime clock by a rule called the *Regiment of the Night Hours*. Instruments for reading this clock, called "nocturnals," date from the late thirteenth century. In addition, there were tables for calibrating it by half-month intervals. It is not clear from the *Journal* just what role this clock may have played in Columbus's navigation. [32]

The ship's clock, which insured the equal division of labor, was the main timekeeper. [33] The day was divided into four-hour watches, during which different teams (watches) of seamen operated the ship. A ship's boy [34] on each watch turned the half-hour sand glass (*ampolleta*) each time the load stopped flowing. Immediately he rang a gong to announce the turn of the glass, and shouted out some ditty. [35] Normally courses were changed at the change of watch, doubling the number of hands who could readily be brought to bear. [36]

It is not clear if the ship's clock was kept running uniformly until the ship came home and the crew was discharged, or whether it was reset periodically to local sun time.

A third level of timekeeping was required for

Measuring Ship's Speed

The ship's speed was estimated by the pilot, or under his supervision. It required the ability to estimate short time intervals. It seems it was done this way: [37] At the start of the voyage a fixed distance (probably 50 palms, about 40.60 English feet) was marked along the rails. At each bell (possibly less frequently) the pilot checked the ship's speed using a ditty to count the time it took some flotsam or froth to float the distance between the rail markings. [38] Using a conversion table, [39] or an arithmetic rule, he converted the time count to miles per hour. In the late eighteenth century, Captain William Bligh reported that his company preferred this method to the "log and line" technique, which was forbidden on company ships. [40]

Columbus probably counted in "moments", an Italian unit of one-third second. [41] With a 50-palm rail distance and a 5,000-palm mile, the ship's speed (in gmph, "geometric miles per hour") is 108 divided by the count in "moments." For example, 18 moments => 6 gmph; 12 moments => 9 gmph. [42] Columbus's flagship averaged 5.53 ± 2.78 gmph on the outbound voyage to America; Niña averaged 5.95 ± 2.90

gmph homebound to the Azores. Speeds were estimated to integer units. Speeds up to 9 gmph were probably acceptably accurate. However, the higher speeds recorded in the *Journal* may be overestimated by 1-2 gmph.

For instance, the *Journal* says the flagship made 12 gmph on 11 October 1492, implying a count of 9 moments for the froth to move the 50-palm rail distance. At 11 gmph, the theoretical count is 9.8 moments; at 13 gmph, 8.3 moments. Variations in the counting habits of pilots, not to mention sea conditions at the time, could account for this range of 1½ moments (½-second), and make the pilot think he was traveling faster or slower than true. [43] The situation is even worse in the case of Niña, who is said to have run at 14 gmph for the 11 hours of daylight, 6 February 1493. This rate of speed implies a pilot count of 7.7 moments, hardly distinguishable from the count for 13 gmph. [44]

Recording Progress Measurements

The pilot recorded the ship's change in position on a plotting board, or directly on his voyage map, [45] using dividers. One name for the plotting board was the *toleta del marteloio*, "gridiron of the hammering (gong-ringing)." [46] The original design looks just like the rhumb network on a nautical chart, the "gridiron," but without the outlines of ocean basins and landmasses. [47] It was used at the ringing of the ship's gong or bell. The principle winds were sometimes included, but were unnecessary adornments. With north at the top and east to the right, it was easy enough for the initiated to box the compass. The scale of miles was often omitted. It is not absolutely essential as it is on the charts, where land masses are drawn to a specific scale. The user could apply any scale which suited his needs. [48] The *toleta* is quite important in the history of technology — an analog computer for solving problems in vector analysis. Equivalent computational devices and polar graphs are still in use.

John Rotz describes how to use the *toleta* in his *Boke of Idrography* of 1542. [49] The pilot multiplied the estimated ship's speed by the time since the last speed measurement to obtain the distance traveled. Then he opened the dividers by an amount proportional to the distance estimate using some convenient mile scale unit. Setting one foot of the dividers on his previously marked position, he pricked the ship's present position by laying the second foot down along a line parallel to the rhumb sailed. The center of the network might be taken as the ship's relative position a dawn, or at dusk. [50]

Theoretical Course Made Good

Every half- or full-day, typically at dawn or at dusk, the pilot obtained his "course made good" for the period by measuring the distance and bearing between the end points of the traverse marked on the *toleta*. The "resolved" course data were transferred to his nautical chart. The half- or full-day summary might also be recorded in a journal or log book, along with other pertinent data on the ship's progress, events, and observations. After "pricking the chart," the pilot erased the lines and dots on the *toleta* in preparation for recording the next traverse.

Some see little evidence that Columbus used a *toleta*. [51] For the first voyage outbound, the *Journal* records 24-hour summaries for 26 days, and ½-day summaries for five days. On the remaining two days it records bearings and distances at the time of changes in course. Homebound, running close-hauled into the wind a good part of the time, only two 24-hour summaries are recorded; on 15 days half-day summaries are recorded; on 14 days progress is recorded at change in course.

With no change in course or sailing conditions Columbus might prick his voyage map directly with no need for intermediate vector calculations. To obtain the *Journal* summaries for 20, 21 and 23 September, and perhaps for 9 September 1492, when the course was changed some number of times, the *toleta* may have been essential.

In the West Indies, Columbus probably plotted his course on a *toleta*, sketching thereon outline maps of the coasts he passed. With the larger scale more details could be included than on the voyage map. The *Journal* gives examples of the Admiral keeping a running graphical account of his relative position. The most convincing occurs between dawn 19 November and 10 a.m. 20 November when the fleet ran some 25 leagues NEbyN of Bahía de Tánamo (*Puerto del Principe*), well out of sight of land, a little north of Brown's Bank. The *Journal* notes that they were some 12 leagues from Isabela. [52] Columbus could not have known this unless he had been plotting his course on a *toleta*, on his voyage map, or both. [53]

The Raxon de Marteloio

Modern writers tend to give more space to the trig tables associated with the *toleta* than to the *toleta* itself. The tables almost certainly derive from the *toleta*. They, and rules for using them, are called the *raxon del marteloio*, literally, "reckoning of the hammering." They list pairs of sides of various right triangles, one side of unit length, with one of the angles varying from 0 to 8 compass points. The *raxon* is a method of similar triangles for figuring how far a ship is off course, and how to regain that course. As Andrea Bianco puts it: "This is the mastery of navigation by the raxon de marteloio, as revealed by this 'circle and square,' [54] and by the *toleta*, by which we may know things like the *toleta* does, by heart (*a mente*), and know how to go to all parts of the world without scale and without dividers." [55]

This memorized digital technique is much more difficult to learn and to use than the *toleta* — and far more subject to error. Andrea Bianco warned potential users: "Realize that any person who wishes to make use of this *raxon*, now here, now there, has to know how to multiply and divide well." Since Bianco's tables contain errors, he may not have used the technique himself. [56]

Verifying the Ship's Theoretical Position

The *Journal* says Columbus "ordered that at sunrise and sunset the vessels should join him, because these two times are when the atmosphere provides the opportunity to see farthest." [57] The crew could see at least one "kenning" ahead, about 21 statute miles. [58] This action was a safety precaution for night sailing in strange waters. The flagship averaged under 4 knots, so they could sail over the waters seen at sunset until about midnight before having serious concerns about running aground. Before leaving the Canaries Columbus instructed his captains not to proceed under sail after midnight once they had gone 700 leagues to the west. [59] This order was never executed. [60] Columbus was more concerned that land might not be found unless the risk was taken.

With the ships drawn together, the officers pooled their opinions about their actual position and expectations. The *Journal* records several comparisons of estimates of position. [61] The limitations of the *toleta* were understood, at least intuitively. To complete the picture, observations of natural phenomena (water conditions, sea life, star and sun positions, and so forth.) were compared to expectations for the apparent progress of the voyage. The *Journal* is particularly rich in examples of this sort. The following case is probably the best.

Columbus: Class "A" Navigator?

Landfall, homebound, was made on 15 February 1493. Some pilots thought it was Madeira, others, *Roca de Sintra* near Lisbon. Columbus located them way back in the Azores. His prediction was verified on 18 February by the inhabitants of Santa María island. Columbus made a note of his predictive accuracy, "although he was making it [that is, estimating his position] somewhat beyond." [62] Las Casas added, "he says that he pretended to have gone a greater distance to confuse the pilots and sailors who were charting their course so that he would remain the master of the route to the Indies." [63] Would Columbus brazenly write of withholding the route to the Indies in the *diario de a bordo* he was about to give his Queen? Given the wealth of information in the *Journal* from which to reconstruct the route, Las Casas 's statement stands out as a gross misunderstanding — like his misinterpretation of Columbus's "public" and "private" distance estimates discussed further along. At any rate, some see here a Columbus with fabricated pretensions. Did Columbus invent the prediction, or is his a reasoned position. And, in what sense might he have been a superior navigator, if at all?

Reconstruction of his voyage track (his dead reckoning) on a contemporary chart, using data in the *Journal*, puts Columbus close to Madeira on 15 February, "somewhat beyond" Santa María — actually some 110 geometric leagues to the southeast. On 10 February Columbus 's dead reckoning was running about 60 geometric leagues behind the other pilots' estimates, but on about the same parallel. So, his dead reckoning did not differ much from his mates's. However, he thought he was actually an additional 90 geometric leagues behind them, to the south of Flores in the Azores, and near the parallel of Cape St. Vincent in 37°N Lat. How Columbus refigured his position sets him apart from his mates.

He reasoned that they were 263 geometric leagues outbound from Hierro in the Canaries the first time they saw seaweed. [64] This sighting defined the eastern edge of the Sargasso Sea. Homebound they crossed the Sargasso once more, in the opposite direction. On 10 February it had been three days since they had last seen weed, so Columbus figured they must now be out of the Sargasso. Subtracting the easterly progress they had made since that time from the 263 geometric leagues, put them south of Flores on his map — the most westerly of the Azores. This reasoning gave him his longitude.

Columbus's dead reckoning put them on the parallel of Casablanca on 10 February, at 32.5°N Lat. On 3-4 February he thought the North Star was quite high, as on the parallel of Cape St. Vincent, at 37°N Lat. Also, it was getting colder. So he figured he was somewhat north of his dead reckoning. At the time he was probably at about the 36th parallel.

Little wonder Columbus put landfall in the Azores on 15 February. [65]

Establishing the Course for the Coming Watches

This decision falls out naturally from the estimate of current position relative to the expectations of the voyage to that point, and to local conditions. For instance, starting about 20 September 1492, the winds began to shift, forcing them to run northwesterly. The wind changed enough by the 24th to run west again, but at a slightly higher latitude.

At sunset the 25th Martin Alonso Pinzon, *Pinta's* captain, was certain he saw land to the southwest. Everyone else had the same vision. They zigzagged southwest and west through the following afternoon, "until they recognized that what they had been saying was land was not land but sky.

Pilotage

Within sight of land the navigator has landmarks, "hard" points of reference, from which to maintain his bearings — if he can recognize them. "Hire a pilot who knows the waters" is the oft-repeated advice in a fifteenth-century pilot book. [66] The seriousness of the pilot's responsibilities are attested in contemporary marine law. A pilot could be beheaded without benefit of tribunal for ignorance of the waters he claimed to know well. [67]

Atlantic pilots could be hired in Cadiz and other ports. Local pilots were essential for Mediterranean vessels entering the foreign waters of the Atlantic. [68] Pilot books were available for do-it-yourself mariners. They had information on tides, shoals, depths and bottoms, channels, landmarks, bars and reefs, leading marks, port facilities, and so forth. [69] But they were really quite inadequate, both in extent and accuracy. And surviving contemporary charts were too small-scale to have been practical for pilotage. Pilots with local knowledge were really the only practical answer.

The drop lead is basic to pilotage. Atlantic and north European mariners developed a skill at finding their way in French, English and Baltic waters using soundings and the type of bottom material brought up. This type of information was particularly valuable when approaching the English Channel and the northern half of the Bay of Biscay in haze or fog. The *Journal* records numerous cases of Columbus sending the ships' boats inshore to probe the depths and bottoms of harbors, inlets and river mouths.

Columbus gave brief evaluations of the harbors he visited. He noted that the tide at Bahía de Tánamo (*Puerto del Principe*) is high at the same local sun time it is low at Palos. [70] The *Journal* preserves his detailed description of Acul Bay (*La Mar de Sancto Thomé*), written in the style of contemporary pilot books. [71] This and other data preserved in the *Journal* are prime data for the pilot book the Prologue says Columbus planned to prepare. [72] It is unknown if he ever prepared it.

Post-Voyage Analysis

This analysis may be done on several levels. On the lowest, the data from the voyage enters into a growing database on the regions visited, a practice continued into modern times. [73] These data, combined with those from other voyages, are incorporated in updated charts, pilot books, climatological tables, and so forth, for subsequent use by mariners. At the highest level the data enters into the planning process for the next voyage. Many of these considerations were discussed earlier under the title "Pre-Voyage Planning and Route Strategy."

Among the most important results of this analysis was the course strategy for the return to Hispaniola. Columbus's voyage chart would have told him to run southwest some 900 leagues to the point where he left Hispaniola. A westerly course would take him into the Bahamas near his first landfall. A west southwest course would take him into unknown waters south of Hispaniola. This course strategy is discussed at length later, under the title "Columbus: Dedicated Magnetic 'Compass and Chart' Navigator."

How Long Was Columbus's League?

Introduction

Reckoning the length of Columbus's league [74] is a problem in historical metrology, an arcane subject which tracks how standards of measurement were established, controlled, modified, and passed on. This study is driven principally by archaeologists' measurements — lengths of measuring sticks, dimensions of monuments, distances between mileposts, and so forth. Documents citing equivalences between units (for example, so many feet per mile), their institution and use, and so forth, round out the picture by permitting the size of units which have not survived monumentally to be calculated. This is a subject dominated by numbers, formulas, and calculations.

Few Columbanists are concerned with Columbus's league. It is needed principally to trace his routes and to locate his first landfall in America. The *Journal* contains the needed course data, physical dimensions of islands, and other geographical distances, expressed in leagues or miles. To track his routes correctly one must know how his units of length relate to the modern nautical mile (NMi).

Most opinions about Columbus's league derive from incompletely modeled reconstructions of his first voyage, or from incorrect contemporary theories of the size of the earth. The principal difficulty has been to trace his league to a documented standard.

Roman Mile Hypothesis.

On the authority of Fox (1882), Markham (1893,18,n.2), Nunn

(1924,18), DaCosta (1939,210), Morison (1942; 1963), [75] and so forth, most writers assert Columbus used the Roman mile of about 4853 English feet, [76] and a league of four Roman miles, about 3.19 nautical miles (NMi). [77] DaCosta identifies this league with Azurara's *légua maritima Portuguesa*, and Diogo Gomes's *légua de Lisboa*, adopting the name "Portuguese maritime league" (PML). [73] The contemporary "league of Bourgogne" is unambiguously equivalent to 4 Roman miles. [79] So is the Arab *parasang* of 3 Arab miles. [30] Franciscus Becharius's chart of 1403 (Yale) has a mile scale labeled *Spaenss mylen*, "Spanish miles," of 17½ to the meridian degree. [81] Sixteenth-century writers refer without distinction to the Spanish and the Portuguese league. Apparently this unit of measure circulated widely in maritime Europe and North Africa, whatever its name. Here it is called simply the *gran legua*, "big league."

As DaCosta puts the argument for the Roman mile hypothesis, [82] Columbus, an Italian, surely used the Italian mile, the hand-me-down mile of the Romans. He himself said he used a league of four miles. [83] The Portuguese were using a league unit as early as the thirteenth century. [34] Having sailed with the Portuguese, Columbus was familiar with their leagues. These associations suggest the hypothesis.

This argument is more *persuasio* than proof that Columbus might have used the Roman mile and *gran legua*. Charlier (1987 and 1988,117-24) gives an interesting alternate, but inconclusive, argument based on a single statistic.

The Long League Hypothesis.

Some sixteenth-century cosmographers, like Chaves, Medina, and Cortes, specify a mariner's league of 17½ to the meridian degree. This definition suggests it was 3.43 NMi long. In 1524, the *Junta de Badajoz* made it official. Gelcich (1885), among others, proposed this may be Columbus's league. But it suffers from being a paper standard, as well as from being too long.

In his *Regimiento de Navegacion* (Madrid 1606), Garcia de Cespedes noted that in Spain "some give 15 Spanish leagues [to the meridian degree], others 16, and the most common, 17½, and others, 18, and others more." [85] Did Spanish mariners use several standards, each of a different length with respect to the true length of the meridian degree (60 NMi)? Surely the confusion among mariners in the same work pool would have been intolerable.

There is a different explanation. The size of the earth was only known approximately before 1617 when Snellius published his measurements, short by 3.5%. Earlier, cosmographers looked to the classics. Those influenced by Eratosthenes saw the meridian degree as 17½ leagues long; under Posidonius's sway, 16²/₃; under Ptolemy, 15²/₃. And so on. These are Cespedes' figures without the fractional parts. It has been suggested that the choices may connect to Portugal's and Spain's territorial politics. But in all these cases it seems to be the same *gran legua* of four Roman miles.

General caution: Virtually every sixteenth-century league defined in terms of the meridian degree must be incorrect. [86] The lengths of these leagues in modern units cannot be calculated from their definitions by substituting the twentieth century value of the meridian degree. The one probable exception involves units tied to the meridian degree of 56²/₃ Arab miles, say 18.9 *grandes leguas*. [87] Unfortunately, this caution is often ignored. The true lengths of these leagues must be learned from measurements of surviving measuring sticks, monuments, and the like, through rules of equivalence given in commercial, legal, and scientific documents.

Short Mile Hypotheses

A few researchers have calculated Columbus's first landfall in America from his transoceanic course data. More recently Peck (1991) and Knox-Johnston (1992) have reported on using their small sailboats as analog computers for reconstructing Columbus's track.

These studies vary significantly in assumptions made, and first landfalls predicted. They do have one thing in common: They show that the Roman mile and *gran legua*, and any larger units, would have moved Columbus well to the west of the eastern margin of the Bahamas — into Florida, central Cuba, and beyond. Fox, Morison, and others attribute this excess to Columbus overestimating his progress each day.

Pragmatists recover from theory by recalculating with a "league" just small enough to avoid overshooting the eastern Bahamas. Here are lengths of "leagues" experimenter's used to make their calculations "work out:" Schott (1882), 2.835 NMi; Gelcich (1885), 2.3 NMi; [88] McElroy (1941), and Fuson and Treftz (1976), 2.89 NMi; Marden (1986), 2.57 NMi.

Judge (1986) and Marden (1986), influenced by Schott, believe they have found the historical basis of Columbus's league in the works of Bourne (1574) and Blundeville (1606). Englishman Bourne asserts (indirectly) that the Spanish and Portuguese used a league of 2.82 NMi, just Schott's experimental result. [89] However, since Marden overshot with this "league," he shortened it some 9% to 2.57 NMi. Richardson and Goldsmith (1987), using the 2.82 NMi league, but somewhat different assumptions, put Columbus's landfall right off San Salvador, instead of Samana Cay. [90]

Bourne's 2.82 NMi league is really a mathematical fiction to give his English clients a way to convert the scales of French, Spanish and Portuguese charts to the English league. The league scales on these charts were normalized to Eratosthenes's short meridian degree of 17½ *grandes leguas*. Bourne assumed there were 20 English leagues of 15,000 feet to the meridian degree. [91] His assumption implies a meridian degree of 49.3 NMi, instead of 60 NMi — almost 18% too small. 17½ *grandes leguas* of 4 Roman miles are only 55.9 NMi — almost 7% too small. [92]

McElroy (1941) also calculated the homebound leg of the first voyage. He needed a significantly smaller "league" of 2.70 NMi to do so. Important principle: If your methodology cannot retrace Columbus's homebound course correctly, its application to the outbound voyage is suspect.

None of these numerical experiments is definitive. Too little is yet known of the forces which acted upon Columbus's ship in October, 1492, to say nothing of certain aspects of his navigation still debated. [93] One thing seems clear, however: Columbus's effective league, if not his actual league, was smaller than the *gran legua*, probably lying between 2.3 and 2.87 NMi.

The Geometric League

Mediterraneans used a short marine league of 2.67 NMi, about ⁵⁄₆th the *gran legua*, the geometric league, of four geometric miles of 5,000 palms of 13.5 Roman digits. This mile is represented in the scales of most Italian and Catalan nautical charts of the period. Wagner (1895, 1900) isolated it statistically, and showed it was well-defined historically. [94] In the Becharius chart cited earlier, this short mile is contrasted with the Spanish and Dutch leagues, and with the degree of latitude. Direct measurements from a large photo put these units in approximately these ratios: Dutch league : Spanish league : 4 Chart miles :: ⁶⁄₅ : 1 : ⁵⁄₆ These scales are normalized to the false meridian degree of 17½ Spanish leagues, that is *grandes leguas*.

The short mile is so fundamental to Columbus's maritime origins it is difficult to believe he was unfamiliar with it. Did he actually use it on his first voyage to America? D'Albertis (1893) considered he used something close to it, namely, a league of 2.664 NMi. The evidence is indirect.

Outbound, the Admiral gave the crew numerically smaller progress estimates than his own. Las Casas says they were bogus figures, concocted to allay fears should the voyage be long. How could he fool the crew? The fleet had at least five practicing Spanish pilots who would know the truth. Was there a conspiracy of silence among them?

If the Admiral really used the smaller league, his estimates of progress would be numerically larger than the Spaniards'. Converting his to the Spanish units for comparison is reasonable considering how the small daily differences would mount. If this hypothesis is true then one would expect to find the ratio of ⁵/₆ths in comparisons between Columbus's and his pilots' estimates.

In fact, the progress estimates Columbus gave the crew average ⁵/₆ths of his own estimates. Since the individual ratios are not all precisely ⁵/₆ths some reject this example. [95] Yet, on 1 October, the Admiral's pilot estimated they made 578 leagues from Hierro. Columbus told the crew 584 leagues, but recorded 707. Note that 584 is approximately ⁵/₆ths of 707. If one counters that Columbus and/or the pilot were not very accurate at estimating distance, then how does one explain that on 19 September the pilots of the three ships and Columbus were consistently close in their estimates of 440, 420, 400, and 420 leagues, respectively? [96]

But, did Columbus really use the geometric league? The unit was basic to his early maritime experience. The hypothesis is consistent with *Journal* data and numerical experiments. Since the *gran legua* and longer leagues move the fleet well beyond the Atlantic margin of the Bahamas, is there another possibility?

Perhaps Columbus's Progress Figures Are Phony

It has been suggested that Columbus deliberately concocted the anomalous data in the *Journal* to keep the location of the discoveries secret. [97] The *Journal* contains 37 Roman numerals, over 400 Arabic numerals, and more than 500 word numerals. Surely some figures would be incorrect, even without deliberate falsifications. After all, the data in the *Journal* is the offspring of at least three hands. But the possibility that Columbus "created" his progress estimates raises serious questions about his rationality.

Deliberately overestimating his outbound daily progress by some 9% makes no sense. They would guarantee a competitor following the *Journal* would find the Indies. A smarter strategy: underestimate daily progress to discourage a would-be interloper from going much beyond the shorter distance.

Just what of importance could Columbus have hidden from anyone? At least five other, technically competent, navigators survived the voyage. Four other survivors were probably also capable pilots. The *Journal* records he conferred with these men about the fleet's position on several occasions, with comparable results.

If the data in the original *diario* Columbus gave the Queen was so incorrect, why did he save his copy of this "cooked book" for posterity's contempt? What value did it have if he had his correct, but secret, copy? Why did he not throw it overboard on the second voyage?

Columbus a Quadrant Navigator?

Early Astronomical Navigation

Since Homer's time mariners have used the pole star, the Big and Little Dippers, and the sun to estimate their relative northing or southing. [98] The navigator memorized the position of the pole star in the rigging, or relative to a spear or body parts, for each of a few key ports or headlands. [99] Homebound, on 3 February 1493, Columbus made just such a non-instrument observation of the North Star relative to Cabo San Vicente. [100] This knowledge of North Star altitudes was exploited by sailing parallels of latitude. The strategy: sail north or south to the parallel of the destination port. Then zigzag east or west down the parallel to land, winds permitting, adjusting the course from new star sights. [101] The magnetic compass let the mariner sail several days in overcast weather between star sights. [102] The astrolabe and quadrant [103] permitted greater accuracy in estimating latitude. Correction rules, the "Regiment of the North Star," were introduced to account for the North Star's orbit around the celestial pole.

The Portuguese exploited the sun's noon altitude to estimate latitude below about 10°N Lat., where the North Star becomes fuzzy and finally disappears from view. This technique required extensive tables of the sun's declination, and eight rules for converting the sun's measured altitude to latitude. Astronomers Abraham Zacuto and Johanes Müller (Regiomontanus) had already updated the solar tables needed. [104]

The sixteenth century introduced additional navigation rules to solve the spherical triangle problem: Given the latitude of the start and end of a run along a constant bearing, what is the distance traveled and the difference in longitude? The surviving navigation literature emphasizes these new techniques, often criticizing mariners, but without adequately describing their methods. The emphasis on the "new" obscures the fact that the older techniques still thrived.

The principal issue: Is it true, as popularly believed, that Columbus used the quadrant or astrolabe to determine his latitude at sea during his first voyage so he could sail precisely due west? Columbus was well-positioned to have used the instruments as posited. The record suggests he did not do so.

Arguments That Columbus Used the Astrolabe or Quadrant for Navigation

A copy of Zacuto's *Almanach perpetuum* exists in the Colombino,

Seville, the remains of Columbus's library. Columbus knew of an eclipse of the moon in time to play magician with Jamaican natives on 29 February 1504. Thus, he may have had with him a copy of Regio-montanus's *Ephemerides Astronomicae*. [105] In possession of such works, Columbus surely knew how to figure latitude from the noon altitude of the sun. Probably starting with Humboldt, the idea has spread that Columbus had a copy of the *Ephemerides* aboard the flagship, and must have made use of it on the first voyage. [106] But, where is the direct evidence? Francisco Albo, Magellan's pilot, practiced the new navigation with the mariner's astrolabe. Virtually every entry in his journal contains a statement like this: "On Thursday, 5th of the said [January, 1520], the sun was 81°30' high, with 21°19' of declination, from which our separation from the line was figured at 29°49', and the course was SWbyS." [107] There is no statement in the *Journal* even remotely similar to this one.

Taylor (1957,167) argues that Columbus ran down the parallel of the Canaries to the New World guided by quadrant readings of the North Star: Columbus learned how to navigate in Portugal, where he learned the latest techniques. [108] Dr. Chanca wrote that some pilots on the second voyage "knew how to go from Spain and back by the North Star." [109] Thus, the technique was becoming common. Further, on his third voyage Columbus himself ran down the latitude of Sierra Leone making daily observations of the North star. [110]

Taylor's argument takes "possibility" for "fact," holding that Columbus's prior knowledge and later use make it credible to believe Columbus navigated with the quadrant on his first voyage. Is it a case of wanting to believe Columbus's navigational practice was on the cutting-edge of new developments?

Contrary Evidence and Rebuttals

"Yo navegaba en el paralelo de Canaria," recalled Columbus in 1498. [111] Even so, there is direct evidence that his run down the parallel was not guided by quadrant readings. The only records of his use of the quadrant on the first voyage are these: 2 Nov, 42°N; 21 Nov, 42°N; 13 Dec, 34°N. His actual latitudes were 21.°1N (*Puerto de Mares*), 21.°5N (between Cuba and Acklins Island), and 19.°1N (*Puerto de la Concepción*), respectively. With results this bad — twice he was moored in protected anchorages — is it credible to believe Columbus could, or would, use a quadrant to navigate along a parallel on the open ocean?

But the *Journal* says San Salvador is on the same latitude as Hierro in the Canaries. Columbus must have measured its latitude with the quadrant just as the Portuguese were in the habit of doing wherever they landed. It is not trivial that the *Journal* actually says San Salvador "island is on an east-west line with the island of Hierro." [112] A due-west magnetic compass course would also produce an "east-west line" on Columbus's chart. [113] Because of magnetic variation, his actual track might well have been bent some distance from the latitude of Hierro in 28°N Lat. Indeed, modern San Salvador, generally thought to be Columbus's first landfall, is in 24°N Lat. A 4° error in reading a quadrant on land would hardly recommend Columbus as an expert in its use.

To preserve the illusion, Morison (1941) suggests Columbus really shot the wrong star while in Cuba and Hispaniola. This explanation implies Columbus was unable to distinguish a 27-story building from a 12-story building while standing 300 feet away. After looking at the North Star for four months relative to the flagship's rigging, and with it gradually approaching the horizon as he moved south, is it reasonable to believe Columbus would mistake the position of Polaris at such a high elevation, and on three separate occasions?

Other commentators suggest Columbus deliberately substituted the wrong figures to hide the location of the Indies and avoid a conflict between Spain and Portugal. [114] However, the *Journal* says first landfall was due west of the Canaries, inferentially near 28°N Lat. The *Journal* also says they turned south from the first landfall into lower latitudes, not north. Columbus even repudiated his poor results of 21 November. He decided something was wrong with the quadrant, and put it away until he could fix it on land. [115]

Columbus: Dedicated "Compass and Chart" Navigator

Many hints suggest Columbus was a dedicated "compass and chart" navigator. For instance, the immediate objective of his second voyage was to relieve his men at Navidad on the north coast of Hispaniola. Did he angle south some 8° from the Canaries to the latitude of Navidad, and then sail west along the twentieth parallel to Hispaniola? Passenger Michael de Cuneo wrote "Our course was WbyS." [116] This statement contrasts with Dr. Chanca's that there were pilots with the fleet who could "go from Spain and back by the North Star." Regardless, they followed Columbus down the WbyS rhumb this time out.

Instead of Hispaniola or Puerto Rico, they fell in with the island of Dominica at about 16°N. Why? The cynic suggests Columbus was playing with the lives of his men at Navidad, and with the colonists in his fleet, to do a bit of discovering along the way. Alternatively, a westerly variation of the magnetic compass, plus a current set and leeway with southerly components, probably bent the fleet's track southward from their WbyS course. [117]

How did Columbus determine to sail WbyS? Lay a straight-edge on a flat map of the first voyage track. [113] A WbyS course of 850 geometric leagues ends 60 geometric leagues due east of his point of departure for home from Samana Bay, Hispaniola, and just north of where he placed the island of Matinino on 16 January 1493. [119] A westerly course would have lead to San Salvador again. A WSW course would have run some 950 geometric leagues into unknown waters, to a point 215 geometric leagues due south of eastern Hispaniola. WbyS was the only reasonable constant-bearing course Columbus could have taken to return to Hispaniola on his second voyage. [120]

On the third voyage in 1498, Columbus told his commodores to follow his second voyage track. In particular, from the Canaries to Dominica they were to "sail to the WbyS for 850 leagues." [121] WbyS became the standard course to the Indies for years afterward. It even manifests itself in La Cosa's planisphere of ca. 1500. [122]

If Columbus and the Spaniards navigated by the North Star, why did Columbus not give them instructions like this: "Sail SW to 16°N Lat., and then run west down that parallel to Dominica?"

How Might Columbus Have Realized Such Gross Latitude Errors?

There were many designs for quadrants in Columbus's day. The simplest and most common design was the *Quadrans vetus* of John of Montpellier. In the late thirteenth century rabbi Jacob ben Machir (Profacius) of Marseilles wrote a treatise on a new design called the *Quadrans novus*. [123] Quite sophisticated mathematical and astronomical calculations could be accomplished on this analog computer. The existence of these advanced designs in the thirteenth century suggests the quadrant Columbus used on the first voyage may not have been the simple *Quadrans vetus* still used by seamen in the sixteenth century.

By 1532 Peter Apian had published a design called the *Quadrans astronomicus*. [124] The feature of interest is this quadrant's shadow scale (labeled *umbra recta* and *umbra versa*), sometimes called the *scala altimetra*. It is moved from the typical box-scale at the quadrant's vertex to just inside the periphery, next to the elevation, or latitude, scale. In addition, it has been decimalized from the old Roman duo decimal units. [125] It so happens that 42 units on the *scala altimetra* correspond to 22° on the latitude scale, and 34 units on the *scala altimetra* correspond to 19°. Recall that Columbus read 42°N Lat. when he was actually in 21.°1N Lat. and 21.°5N Lat., respectively, and 34°N Lat. when he was actually in 19.°1N Lat. It would seem Columbus's quadrant may have had the shadow scale arranged as in Apian's quadrant.

But how did he read the wrong scale? While sighting the North Star along the fiducial edge of the quadrant he brought the thumb of his free hand into position to clamp the weighted thread against the periphery. In the flickering lamplight he seems not to have noticed his thumb covered the numeral on the latitude scale, leaving visible the adjacent numeral on the *scala altimetra*. [126]

How Well Could Columbus Measure Latitude with a Quadrant?

It is often assumed that the quadrant is easy to use accurately. Geoffrey Chaucer's leads us to believe it was within the capability of a 10-year old. [127] What was Columbus's true skill with the instrument? The surviving records of his first and third voyages, and related materials, are suggestive.

Without entering into details, there is no indication Columbus tried to measure the sun's altitude with any instrument during the first three voyages. He did attempt to take the height of the North Star with a quadrant, more successfully on the third voyage. He recognized that the North Star orbits the celestial pole, but thought that the diameter of the orbit was larger near the equator (about 10°) than in the area of the Sargasso Sea and Azores (about 5°). [128] The orbit's true diameter was just under 7° at the time. Could he have been familiar with the "Regiment of the North Star" [129] in 1498 and still believe the diameter of the orbit varied by 5°? These data suggest that by 1498 Columbus's range of measurement error may have been ±2° or ±3°, a little better than Portuguese researcher Mestre Joan's apparent skill at sea in 1500.

Early Portuguese Experiments Measuring Latitude and Star Positions

Just how skilled were late fifteenth-century Portuguese seamen at measuring latitudes at sea — especially those who sailed around Africa?

The most efficient routes to South Africa required sailing far out into the South Atlantic to take advantage of the prevailing winds, and to avoid the contrary winds of coastal areas. Latitude sailing became most important to avoid getting lost in the South Atlantic and Indian Oceans. Since there is no conspicuous star close to the south celestial pole, the Portuguese experimented with exploiting circumpolar constellations and the sun to determine latitude. In the early 1480's a procedure was worked out, with associated tables, for determining latitude from the sun. [130]

During the summer of 1499, Vasco da Gama returned to Lisbon from opening a trade route to India by rounding Africa. Wishing to exploit this route without delay, King D. Manuel sent a new fleet of 12-14 ships and some 1200 men back to India under the command of Pedro Alvares Cabral. They departed 9 March 1500, shaping the standard course to the Cape Verde Islands, sighting them about 21 March. Continuing south (magnetic), the course recommended by Vasco da

Gama, the westward moving currents and an easterly compass variation sent them across the Atlantic, where they sighted Brazil on 21 April.

A certain Mestre Joan, physician and surgeon, [131] shipped with Cabral. His duties included performing some navigation experiments. His letter to the king is revealing. By happy accident he and two pilots had the opportunity to set up their equipment on Brazil's shore. Taking the sun's altitude at noon, they calculated their latitude as 17°S — probably fairly accurately. [132]

Joan's onboard assignments included making independent estimates of fleet progress, and comparing his assessments with those of the pilots. "All the pilots advance ahead of me, so much so that Pero Escobar [133] leads by 150 leagues, and some more and others less. [134] But who states the truth cannot be determined until, in good time, we will near the Cape of Good Hope, and there we will know who runs more certain, they with the chart, or I with the chart and with the astrolabe." Navigating by the chart alone suggests the Portuguese pilots were purely "compass and chart" navigators.

Joan also had to measure the star positions of the Southern Cross, [135] and to determine which instruments were best for measuring star altitudes at sea. In particular, how well did the *kamal*, lately brought from India by Vasco da Gama, work in practice? Joan complained that space to set up his equipment was at a premium, and what with an infected leg, he could do little aboard ship. "As to how its stars lie situated," he wrote, "as yet I have not been able to determine in which degree each one lies. First, it seems to me to be impossible, at sea, to take the altitude of any star, because I worked hard at it, and however little the vessel rocked, erred 4° or 5° from the means that may be employed on land. [136] And I say almost the same thing of the 'boards of India,' [137] that they [the pilots] are unable to take [altitudes] with them, except with lots of work. If Your Highness would learn how they all disagree on the *pulgadas*, [138] you would laugh, greater [differences] than from the astrolabe. For, from Lisbon as far as the Canaries, each of them disagreed on the number of *pulgadas*. Some were saying more than others by three and four *pulgadas*. [139] And similarly from the Canaries as far as the Cape Verde Islands. And this safeguarding that all who took altitudes did so at the same hour. As to the way most estimated how many *pulgadas* there were — by the length of the course that it seemed to them they had been sailing, not [estimating] the course [distance by the *pulgadas*."

Joan's last statement says the pilots worked backwards to figure latitudes from their estimates of course made good. This procedure unveils Portuguese pilots of 1500 as strictly "compass and chart" navigators. Joan concludes "at sea it is better to be guided by the altitude of the sun than by any star, and better with the astrolabe than with quadrant or with any other instrument."

If the Portuguese of 1500 were not yet taking instrument measurements of latitude at sea as a matter of course, how likely is it Columbus would have been doing so eight years earlier?

Effects on the Maps and Sailing Books [140]

A nautical chart is without value to a pilot unless it supports his mode of navigation. Thus, early nautical charts of the New World should provide insights into the method of navigation in vogue. It seems the first charts of the New World were assembled from sketch maps and voyage logs. It is readily observed that surviving early charts hardly coordinate with the correct latitudes of more than a handful of key places. They seem to have been based almost totally on magnetic compass bearings and distance estimates. They display puzzling distortions which can be explained, at least partially, by the navigation process already described. Understanding these distortions is helpful for interpreting geographic information in the early documents about the New World. Most can be classified in a few groups of which the following are the most serious:

Scale Distortion

Most of the surviving early charts of the New World are additions to standard maps of the Old World. Typically, New World land masses are portrayed too large relative to the Old World — a scale distortion. Why? It seems fifteenth-century cosmographers noticed that the difference between measured latitudes of Old World places were inconsistent with the north-south distances between them on the charts. The comparison assumed a length of the meridian degree, the true value of which was not known at the time. Consistency required either changing the assumption or modifying the chart scales. Cosmographers seem to have chosen the latter, putting their faith in classical estimates of the earth's circumference. New World land masses were added to copies of these improperly scaled charts.

The famous Juan de la Cosa planisphere (ca. 1500) is a case in point. [141] The Old World is scaled to Ptolemy's theory, namely, 15²/₃ *grandes leguas* per meridian degree. The New World section was laid down on a false scale with lately acquired true distances equivalent to about 18.8 *grandes leguas* per meridian degree. Consequently the New World in the La Cosa is, theoretically, some 20% larger than equivalent land masses in the Old World. [142]

However, in this instance the situation may be even more complex. Recent measurements suggest Hispaniola may have been copied from a regional map scaled to a league of about 3 Roman miles (a land sur-veyor's measure?). [143] In this event, Hispaniola in the La Cosa is theor-etically 26.6% too large relative to the Old World.

A scale distortion makes it quite difficult to coordinate the lati-tudes of places in the New World with corresponding places in the Old World. In the La Cosa, for instance, although Dominica is in about the correct latitude relative to Africa, the north coast of Cuba, which is really in about 23°N Lat., is depicted at about 35°N Lat.

New World land masses added to maps of the Old World scaled to Erathosthenes's estimate of the size of the earth, namely, 17½ *grandes leguas* per meridian degree, are, in theory, about 7% too large.

East-West Distortion

Cartographers seem to have keyed the position of New World land masses to the terminus of some standard ocean route. The route to the West Indies runs from Hierro to Dominica, over a middle latitude of about 22°N Lat. [144] Cabot's and subsequent voyages, established a route to Newfoundland from Eire, over a middle latitude near 50°N Lat. Dominica and Cape Race, Newfoundland, are within 200 NMi of the same meridian. But, because of the earth's sphericity, Dominica is actually over 65% further along its parallel from the meridian of west-ern Eire than is Cape Race along its parallel. This is the reason New-foundland is shown so much closer to Europe than Dominica in the La Cosa and most other early charts of North America.

This fact of geometry explains why the early outlines of the Atlan-tic coast of North America are so unrealistically stretched east-west. The large east-west distance between Dominica and Cape Race on these maps leads to a very surprising result when combined with

Magnetic Variation Distortion

The magnetic variation of the compass was about 1½-2 points west in Newfoundland, and ½-1 point west in the central Bahamas in the early sixteenth century. [145] Indications are that the variation may have been as much as 2½-3 points west along the middle Atlantic states. The effect of a westerly variation is this: A voyage northeast (true) along the Atlantic seaboard [146] translates into a magnetic compass course of almost EbyN (compass biased for ½-point E variation). Similarly, a voyage southwest (true) translates into a magnetic compass course of almost WbyS.

This peculiar orientation of the North American coast is evident in most early maps. An important example is Juan Vespucci's of 1526. [147] Juan, nephew of Amerigo Vespucci, America's namesake, was an important member of the Spanish Board of Trade. He examined pilots, made maps and instruments, and the like. Some think his chart was the Spanish *padron*, or standard chart, and represented the best information available. The Vespucci, and maps like it, suggest sixteenth-century maps were still being compiled from magnetic compass course data — not from latitude-longitude measurements.

It is clear that, like scale distortion, magnetic variation distortion of the Atlantic seaboard obscures the latitude identification of places. The Indies tend to be mapped in higher latitudes than true.

Compromise Distortions

The ends of the EbyN-running coastline from Florida and the WbyS-running coastline from Nova Scotia in the Vespucci and similar maps are almost on north-south line, but separated by 8°-9° of latitude. Mapmakers had to decide how to connect the northern to the southern sections once they were convinced they were connected. It was not possible geometrically to preserve distances and magnetic bearings along the coastline from Florida to Cape Race, as well as the relative positions of Florida and Newfoundland. Compromises were required.

John Rotz's atlas of 1542 illustrates one compromise. [148] Rotz's coast from Florida trends eastward — as in the Vespucci map. And his coast from Newfoundland also trends westward. He connected the two sections with a north-trending coastline. His choice: preserve the older coastal outlines of Nova Scotia and the Carolinas.

Gerolamo da Verrazzano's world map of 1529 [149] made a different compromise. His coastline from Florida to Newfoundland is sloped ENE. In this way he averaged out the errors. Surely his brother Giovanni's voyage along the coast told him there is no sudden change in the trend of the coastline as displayed in Rotz's chart.

The mapmaker generally had to compromise when connecting two sections of coastline mapped from voyages coming from opposite directions, or in completing the circuit of a large land mass. The completion of the U.S. coastline and the closing of the western gap in the Gulf of Mexico are examples of the first case. The second case is illustrated by the early shapes of the South American continent.

Latitudes Published in the Sixteenth Century Require Verification

The distortions reflect the growing pains and tensions cartography and navigation underwent in the sixteenth century. Still, it is common to find sixteenth century latitude figures from treatises like Alonso de Chaves's *Mariners' Mirror* being used to locate places of interest on modern maps. [150] After all, Chaves was chief pilot, and produced a *padron*. But, consider that at one point Spanish pilots considered the *padron* to be useless. Some would throw the licensed charts overboard and sail with an older chart — if they could find one. [151]

Access to the best available information hardly insures it is actually used, nor that the "best" is correct. Can Chaves's latitude figures for the southeast coast of the U.S. be taken at face value when he states that Grand Bahama Island "lies 30 leagues east of Cape Canaveral, in Florida?" Santa Cruz's and other maps show this same incorrect configuration and scale in the 1540's. [152] Indeed, comparisons of pilot books and maps suggest a fair share of the information in the books was derived from maps. [153]

The correct theory for representing the mariner's world did not appear until 1569, with the publication of Gerard Mercator's famous map of the world on the projection that bears his name. The shapes of the land masses are not yet just right. And it would take awhile longer before mariners could determine both their latitude and longitude with practical accuracy. But that is another story.

Acknowledgements

Much of the research for this study was performed during the past decade as part of a public and private debate over the location of Columbus's first landfall in America. The argument assumes or implies certain features of Columbus's navigation technology. Among the objectives: Resolve the inconsistencies among these features, both at the logical and at the historical levels.

Certain views have been promoted so vigorously that contrary opinions may be somewhat exaggerated here in reaction. The speculative character of this field of inquiry makes it difficult to say with certainty that a particular opinion is truly correct or not. This study proceeded with the hope that the credibility of each hypothesis might be narrowed by testing its consistency over a wide range of related logical and historical facts and relationships.

To the twenty-five and more men and women who participated actively in this debate, many thanks. Their ideas and criticisms opened pathways that could not have been found without them. Particular thanks are due to Oliver Dunn, David Henige, Donald McGuirk, Arne Molander, Douglas Peck, and Neil Sealey for their long term constructive participation and personal encouragement.

Notes

[1] For other opinions see Gelcich (1885), Nunn (1924), DaCosta (1939), McElroy (1941), Morison (1941, 1942), Hewson (1951), Taylor (1957), Waters (1958), Denoix (1960), Ferro (1987), Charlier (1988), and so forth.

[2] See the journal of a non-mariner patron in Mallett (1967) to appreciate the difference. It is also of interest to compare how Pigafetta (tourist) and Albo (Magellan's pilot), as well as how Keeling (patron) and Bonner (pilot), treat the same voyages. Sources: Obregón (1984), Strachan and Penrose (1971), and so forth.

[3] Jados (1975,141-148).

[4] The *Journal* has been transcribed and translated many times. For example, see Morison (1963), Dunn and Kelley (1989).

[5] Columbus took enough bread and wine for more than a year's voyage, plus seeds with which to raise a crop. He was fairly well supplied with armaments: small cannon (breech-loaded lombards), rifles (spingards), swords, long bows and crossbows, armor, and so forth.

[6] For example, by sending factors ahead, overland, to facilitate diplomatic and financial arrangements, to open markets, and so forth. See Mallet (1967) for related background. Columbus was given letters of passage, an embassy, and an interpreter to smooth the way with foreign rulers.

[7] Two weather tables for the western Mediterranean survive in Egerton ms.73,fo.24^v(British Library). See Kelley, *Charms* (1977).

[8] See, for example, Mallett (1967), Carus-Wilson (1937,1954), Burwash (1947).

[9] Major (1847,110-11), and others.

[10] The warrant for his arrest caused problems in the Azores, homebound.

[11] *Journal*, 6 September 1492.

[12] The *pleito* of Juan of Aragon, cited in Morison (1942,I:194,199n.39). Morison takes the position that the deportation of the Jews hampered and delayed Columbus's departure. It may also be viewed as a covenient smoke screen.

[13] As a second tactic, Columbus might have run a non-standard route to the Canaries, as he did in May, 1498, and approached Gran Canary from the north. But

the narrations of the *Journal* and Ferdinand Columbus are too incomplete to verify this possibility.

[14] The so-called *Ginea Portogalexe*, dated ca. 1489, is representative of the best charts available to Columbus. It can be seen in Egerton ms. 73, fos. 31 and 32, and in expanded form in fo. 36 (British Library). This large collection of charts and essays in fifteenth century Venetian is a prime source of information on nautical matters in Columbus's time.

[15] In addition to Columbus there were his pilot, Peralonso Niño of Moguer, Christobal Garcia Sarmiento and Sancho Ruiz de Gama, the pilots of *Pinta* and *Niña*, respectively, and Bartolome Roldan of the *Niña*, an able seaman possibly apprenticed to Sancho Ruiz. Vincente Anes Pinzon, Captain of *Niña*, kept an independent record of his ship's positions. It is probable that Martin Alonso Pinzon and his brother Francisco, Captain and Master of *Pinta*, respectively, as well as Juan de la Cosa, Master of the flagship, could navigate a ship. Safety dictated that several independent accounts of the voyage be maintained as a hedge against individual estimating errors and the loss of the pilot.

[16] For example, Skelton (1958) reproduces a few explorers' working maps. A map three feet high (north-south) and five feet wide (east-west) could cover an area of about 1,000 by 1,600 geometric leagues, large enough to encompass the 1,200 geometric league distance from the Canaries to the Bahamas.

[17] For example, the mysterious islands of Antilia, Satanazes, Himadoro, Balmar, Brazil, and so forth. On 25 September Columbus and Martin Alonso discussed the possibility that they were near some islands appearing on one of the Admiral's maps. By 1492 the more progressive cosmographic maps had moved Antilia and the other islands much further out into the Atlantic and had made them much smaller than in earlier conceptions, reflecting the fact that no one could find them.

[18] See, for example, Vignaud (1902).

[19] Nuremburg, 1492. See Ravenstein (1908).

[20] See Harrisse (1892,391f). Behaim's globe does place Antilia and another island near the fleet's probable position on 25 September when Columbus and Martin Alonso discussed possible islands nearby.

[21] "The vertical line within a compass-case, indicating the direction of the ship's head." *OED.*

[22] In large Spanish and Portuguese ships of the sixteenth century quite long tillers were used, requiring perhaps 15-20 men to manage it in rough weather.

Tackles were also attached from the tiller's end to eye-bolts in the side walls of the tiller-room. Waters (1958,314).

[23] Apparently two were required on important sixteenth-century Spanish vessels.

[24] 8-9 September 1492. The seas were coming over the bow making it difficult to maintain the course.

[25] Some writers hold that the gimble was not introduced until the fifteenth century. However, the device was known in Europe in the thirteenth century. An example of its use in a hand warmer is given in Villard de Honnecourt's *Sketchbook*. See Bowie (1959,28).

[26] It seems this "wet" compass was known in Europe from the first or second century a.d. Two ceramic bowels excavated near Liria, the mercury mining center of Spain, display an 8-point compass rose in the inside bottom with incriptions around the lips which, taken together, say to fill the bowel with quicksilver and float a magnetized needle or load-stone on it to find one's direction at night or in overcast weather. See Fell (1976). This contrasts with the view that the magnetic compass came to western Europe from China.

[27] In northern waters, where the magnetic compass had limited use, the vessel's wake was often used to maintain a near constant course of a few hundred miles.

[28] Lane (1963).

[29] The existence of secular change in variation was not verified until 1633, by Gresham College professor, Henry Gellibrand. Waters (1958,238).

[30] Strachan and Penrose (1971,68).

[31] In this connection also see Nansen (1911,II:308), Cerezo Martinez (1987), and Goldsmith and Richardson, *Numerical Simulations* (1990).

[32] This earliest of *Regiments* is covered in most works dealing with sixteenth century navigation. See, for example, DaCosta (1939,38-48), who pictures Lull's nocturnal, and Albuquerque (1963,206), who reproduces a contemporary calibration table.

[33] Taylor (1958,116), Balmer (1978,622).

[34] Probably the same boy who kept a check on the helmsman. On important

ships a second boy might be stationed in the fo'c's'le with another sandglass as a check on the performance of the first boy. Morison (1942,I:236).

[35] There were ditties and prayers for almost every shipboard activity. It was the steward's (*despensaro*) job to teach the boys these formulas.

[36] For additional information see Morison (1942), Balmer (1978), and others.

[37] See Kelley, "How did Columbus estimate speed at sea?" (1991). Some writers say the ship's clock had a role in estimating speed, probably because of Leonardo Dati's cosmographic poem, *La sfera* (1401). The verse in question reads: *Bisogna l'oriuolo per mirare Quante ore con un vento siano andati, E quante miglia per ore arbitrare.* Uzielli and Amat (1882,38).

[38] In 1574 Bourne mentions that some mariners know a "part of an houre by some number of wordes." Taylor (1963,237).

[39] Possibly scratched into the ship's rail.

[40] See Hewson (1951,159), Waters (1955,266). Earlier, Captain John Smith wrote that the log line "is not worth the labour to trie it." Smith (1970,55).

[41] See Egerton ms.73,fo.43ᵛ(British Library), inter alia, for the "moment." Other people used ½-second counts.

[42] The 5,000-palm maritime mile, the so-called "geometric" mile, was about 4,060 English feet long; the Iberians used the *gran legua* of 4 Roman miles, equivalent to the *parasang* of 3 Arabic miles. Kelley (1983 and 1987).

[43] See Hewson (1951,159) for a discussion of the problems affecting the accuracy of this method.

[44] The fact that no other speed greater than 12 mph is recorded for *Niña* is further justification for believing the 14 mph is a gross over-estimate.

[45] Two things mitigate against the use of the chart for this purpose. First, nautical charts of Columbus's time were not so readily replacable as modern maps, which are inexpensively printed on paper. The owner would not wish to abuse one by repetitively marking and erasing it. Anyone could make a *toleta* with drawing compass and straightedge. Second, there is the possible problem of scale. In the hypothesized 3 by 5 foot voyage chart of Columbus the scale is about 10 leagues per cm. This is just too small to record and resolve accurately the movement of a vessel undergoing several course and/or speed changes during the day. One needs to use a chart or *toleta* with a larger scale, say 1-2 leagues per cm. However, the resultant

course made good is readily transferred to the smaller scale voyage map.

[46] See *toletum* in Latham (1965).

[47] See, for example, Kreutz (1973,375). An incomplete *toleta* is reproduced in DaCosta (1939,177).

[48] A later design is included in Andrea Bianco's atlas of 1436. He called it the *tondo e quadro*, "circle and square." It includes a scale divided two ways: at the top it is divided into two groups of 20 unlabeled units, probably "miles;" at the bottom it is divided into four 50-mile units, two of which are further divided into 10-mile units. The two different scale units suggest that this toleta was intended not only for recording the changes in course during a trip at sea, but for solving tactical problems (as on the maneuvering board of more recent times). See Taylor (1957, Pl.VIII) and DaCosta (1939,Figure 121) for a reproductions of Bianco's *toleta*. A similar design is given in Egerton ms.73,fo.47ᵛ, in an essay on how to solve course problems using the *raxon de marteloio*.

[49] Winter (1948,25-6).

[50] In later times this recording has been done with chalk on a slate near the helmsman, or with a peg-board on the binacle, called a "traverse board," indicating the course and speed or distance made good during each half-hour. Examples or reproductions of traverse boards can be seen in many maritime museums. See Waters (1958,32-3) and Taylor (1957,196) for pictures, and Smith (1627,14) for a seventeenth-century description.

[51] For example, Ferro (1987).

[52] The tip of South Acklins Island is about 15 leagues from the fleet's probable actual position.

[53] Other examples occur in the entries for 26 November (28ʳ2) and 6 December (33ʳ1-15).

[54] The *tondo e quadro* is a plotting board designed to resolve traverses to eighth-winds (5°.626), apparently of Venetian origin. In surviving examples the "square" is not circumscribed by the "circle," so the rhumbs do not quite define eighth-winds as advertised. For reproductions of Bianco's version see DaCosta (1939,Fig.121), Taylor (1957,Pl.VIII). There is also one in Egerton ms.73,fo.47ᵛ (British Library), reproduced in Campbell (1987,442).

[55] For the Venetian text see Lelewel (1852,II:85-6), DaCosta (1939,357, n.505). This particular sentence is often interpreted as saying the *toleta* is the trig

table (*tavola*) of the *raxon del marteloio*. See, for example, Campbell (1987,442). The text is difficult to understand, witness the rather free Portuguese translation given by DaCosta.

[56] Taylor (1957,141-2) associates with the *raxon de marteloio* an instance of some mariners doing a navigational calculation. Not enough information is given to determine if the mariners were actually applying the raxon.

[57] Dunn and Kelley (1989,53). *Journal*, 7 October.

[58] Waters (1967,23).

[59] Thatcher (1903,I:531,n.2). Morison (1942,I:90) makes the case that Columbus thought the distance from Gomera to Cipangu was 750 leagues. Nunn (1924,27-30) makes similar calculations. However, if Columbus worked from a map or globe similar to Behaim's globe, the estimated distance from Gomera to Cipangu would have exceeded 1200 leagues of 4 Roman miles. On the third voyage, Columbus told his commodores they would be close to land after 850 leagues on a WbyS course from the Canaries to Dominica. Morison (1963,260).

[60] When crossing the Venezuelan Basin on the third voyage, Columbus seems to have had the fleet run *a la corda* (jog on and off) after complines (about 9 p.m.) to avoid the possibility of grounding in the dark in this as yet unexplored sea of many small islands. They averaged about 9 gmph (6 knots) in the strong prevailing wind, so midnight would have been too long to safely depend on what could be seen ahead at sunset.

[61] In later times pilots with a fleet might be reticent about showing their journals to the patron for fear the other pilots might obtain a competitive advantage from the premature revelation of its contents. The owners reviewed these journals after the voyage to evaluate pilots for promotion.

[62] *Aunque se hazia algo delantero* (*Journal*, 63ʳ12). This phrase has been variously translated: "even though he thought himself somewhat farther along" (Dunn and Kelley); "Although I had fixed our position a little beyond its true location" (Fuson); "although he had made it a little farther on" (Jane-Vigneras); "although he had made it somewhat further on" (Morison); "although he made them a little beyond their true situation" (Thacher); "although there had been some delay" (Major).

[63] *Journal*, 18 February (63ʳ15-17).

[64] *Journal* entry of 10 February. Las Casas includes this fact, but not the rest of the reasoning.

[65] For more details see Kelley (1983,1987).

[66] Kretschmer (1909,268-358).

[67] Jados (1975,156-157).

[68] Mallett (1967,224 n.1).

[69] See, for example, *Portolano Rizo*, Kretschmer (1909,420-552). Taylor (1957, 132-133) gives a nice summary.

[70] *Journal*, 18 November.

[71] *Journal*, 24 December.

[72] *Componer un libro, Journal*, 2^{r}2.

[73] Most national hydrographic offices request mariners to submit any and all observations of depths, currents, weather, hazards to navigation, port facilities, political conditions, and so forth, for which they will replace charts and forms used to record the data.

[74] Apparently "league" derives from late Latin *leuca, leuga*, the root *leu-* being Indo-European for "stone" (for example, Welsh *llech* = flat stone), suggesting that the term meant the distance between stone markers, perhaps an hour's walk apart. It was indigenous to the Celtic lands of northern and western Europe. Chardon (1980) gives an historical summary culled from the literature.

[75] Morison consistently translated *milla* in Columbus-related documents as "Roman mile."

[76] This figure is a statistical average "standard" Roman mile. The Roman foot varied in time and place. Before the "standard" was introduced from Egypt via Greece and Etruria a longer foot was in use, implying a mile of around 4880 English feet. But from the third century a.d. a shorter foot came into use, implying a short mile of about 4825 English feet. By Columbus's time the standard Roman foot had fallen into disuse, the short and long feet surviving in commercial measures of western Europe in late medieval times. It is relevant that Opicinus de Canistris, writing in 1338, reported the mile of his time was longer than that of ancient Rome. Almagià (1944,I:97n.5). This comment and Machebey's fundamental work suggest the "Roman mile" in the present context was about 4880 English feet long. Even so, the more familiar "standard" mile is used here to avoid confusion, but without losing anything essential.

77 For more recent discussions see: Cerezo Martinez (1987), Sitters (1987), Fantoni and Ingravalle (1987).

78 DaCosta (1939,213). It is not strictly certain that these named leagues consisted of 4 Roman miles.

79 Source: Machabey (1962,48) and Zupko (1978,141). This league of 18,000 feet of Bourgogne of 33 cm. (Machabey's R4 foot) is numerically equivalent to 4 Roman miles of 4872 English feet, just 0.4% longer than the normalized standard of 4853. See Kelley (1983,102-04) for a summary of Machabey's work relevant to this discussion.

80 Hinz (1955,54,62) says the *parasang* is 3 miles of 1000 fathoms of 199.5 cm., making it 19,635.8 English feet long. Dividing by 4 gives an approximate Roman mile of 4909 English feet, just 1% too long.

81 Kraus (1961,62) reads *Spaenis mylen*. The Germanic *mylen* suggests this scale, another labeled *Duitse mylen*, and a latitude scale, were all added after Becharius's time by some northern owner. These additions are professionally done.

82 DaCosta (1939,210-16). DaCosta's exposition of this theory is among the most lucid.

83 For example, in the *Journal* of his first voyage (3 August, 9 September, 7 October, 11 October, 9 December, and so forth), in postilles in d'Ailly's *Imago Mundi* (Nunn 1924), and in his letter to the Sovereigns of his Third Voyage (Major 1847). The latter examples show that Las Casas did not invent the equivalence as has been asserted.

84 Examples are cited by DaCosta (1939,213), but not always in an unambiguously maritime context.

85 DaCosta (1939,215,n.313).

86 Robert Hues, in his *Tractatus de Globis* of 1594 analyzed all the classical and Arab measurements of the meridian degree. "So great [is the] diversity of opinions concerning the true measure of the earth's circumference," he concluded, "let it be free for every man to follow whomsoever he please" (Waters [1958,193]). Could anyone have had a more knowledgeable opinion 100 years earlier?

87 In the ninth century Calif 'Abdallah al-Ma'mun sent experienced astronomers to the plane of Sindjar to measure the meridian degree. They actually marked off a 1° length on the local meridian, measuring the sun's altitude at two places on the same day. They returned the next year to check the results. This quite scientific

process resulted in an estimate of 56²/₃ Arab miles per degree. Taking the Arab mile as 6,545.3 English feet (= 19,635.8/3) discussed in an earlier note, and converting as appropriate, 56²/₃ Arab miles are 61 NMi, 1.7% high. This is a better result than Snellius's first measurement of the meridian degree.

[88] This figure should be amended to 2.7 NMi because of serious numerical errors in his calculations.

[89] The end of Schott's computed track is between Hogsty Reef and the Plana Cays, 40-50 miles south of Samana Cay. He made some small computational errors, which, when corrected, put the end of his track some 30 miles further to the SW.

[90] See Goldsmith and Richardson (1987), *Reconstructing Columbus's First Transatlantic Track*, for their complete analysis.

[91] Bourne gives this data in his *Almanacke* (1571). See Taylor (1963,90). 15,000 feet is 2500 fathoms. Bourne, assuming 20 English leagues measured the same distance as 17½ *grandes leguas*, computed the length of the *gran legua* as 2857 fathoms (= 20 x 2500 / 17½). It is only this result which appears in his *A Regiment for the Sea* (1574), and which is copied by Blundeville. See Taylor (1963,238), Judge (1986,54-5).

[92] Bourne actually did his clients a great disservice. In effect he told them the Spanish *gran legua* was only 14% longer than the English league, whereas the true figure was more like 30%, that is, a 100 league distance on a Spanish chart is actually 130 English leagues. But by Bourne's rule an English captain would compute it to be 114 English leagues.

[93] Numerical simulations give insights into the details of historic voyages. They may even help disprove conjectures about voyage tracks. Goldsmith and Richardson (1990), *Numerical Simulations of Columbus' Atlantic Crossings*, give a most extensive analysis of the first voyage. They compute some 60 different tracks for various assumptions about length of Columbus's league, magnetic variation, drift currents, winds, and leeway, including tracks for the homebound voyage.

[94] Also see Franco (1957) and Nordenskiöld (1897,16-24) for discussions of the same problem.

[95] See Kelley (1987,Fig.4) for a plot of Columbus's "public" and "private" progress estimates to see how closely they correlate.

[96] For a fuller discussion of this subject see Kelley (1983,1987).

[97] Quite strange reconstructions of the voyage have even been made by dis-

carding the recorded course data and "interpreting" other data in the journal as positional information. Why is this "other" data objectively more credible than the course data?

[98] Because of the precession of the equinoxes, Kochab in the leading edge of the bowel of the Little Dipper was the pole star in Homer's day. The current North Star was then some 8° from the celestial pole. By Columbus's day it had moved to about 3½° of the pole. In 1992 it is approaching ½° of the pole.

[99] See Marcus (1953) for some background.

[100] The sea was too rough for a quadrant reading that day.

[101] In practice the route might have to be round about because of unfavorable wind.

[102] Because of magnetic variation and forces acting on the vessel, use of the magnetic compass was not proof of a due east or due west course.

[103] The quadrant is so-called because it is one-fourth of an astrolabe. Its great attraction: for instruments of comparable size, the quadrant has twice the accuracy of an astrolabe.

[104] How to determine the declination of the sun had been known for at least 1500 years when Columbus made his first voyage (Ptolemy, *Almagest* I,15). Because of precession, tables and calculating instruments had to be updated periodically. There was a standard procedure for determining one's latitude from the sun's noon altitude using an astrolabe (Gunther [1923,V:76-7,178-9]) or a quadrant with special scales (Gunther [1923,II:167]).

[105] Alternatively, it may have been Regiomontanus's *Calendarium*, an illustrated book of lunar eclipses, far simpler to appreciate and use than the *Ephemerides*. Thacher (1903,I:359,II:628-632).

[106] "But unfortunately the large number of notes among his writings, one finds nothing to establish that he had known the procedure for calculating latitudes from the height of the sun." Bensaude (1912,26).

[107] Obregon (1984,139). Albo looked up the declination of 21°19' for the day in tables which covered a period of four years. The calculation: 81°30' - 21°19' - 90° = 29°49'S, was the one of eight which might apply.

[108] In a marginal note to Pierre d'Ailly's *Imago Mundi* (Nunn [1924,10], among others), Columbus says he used a quadrant to estimate the length of the

meridian degree while sailing with the Portuguese. Taylor probably meant "navigate with a quadrant." Surely Columbus the mariner learned something of navigation before being shipwrecked in Portugal at about age 27.

[109] For example, Jane 1988,28-9; Major 1847,27. Taylor assumes this form of navigation was only accomplished using quadrant or astrolabe. As Marcus (1953) amply illustrates, Atlantic seamen had been doing latitude sailing for centuries without quadrant and astrolabe.

[110] "Daily observations" is an assumption. Only 3-4 quadrant observations are recorded, beginning when Columbus ran out of wind after a 120 league run SW from the Cape Verde Islands. See Las Casas's abstract of the third voyage in Thacher (1903,II:374-408).

[111] Major (1847,113).

[112] *Journal*, 13 October, 9ᵛ32-3. It was Las Casas, in a marginal note, who put Guanahani in the latitude (*en el altura*) of Hierro.

[113] See the computer-drawn chart in Kelley (1987,Figure 1).

[114] For example, Magnaghi (1928).

[115] Apparently he could find nothing wrong because he used the quadrant again on 13 December with equally poor results.

[116] See DeCuneo's letter (Morison 1963,210). *La nostra via fu a la quarta de ponente verso lebechio* (*Raccolta* III, ii, 96).

[117] Morison (1963,263 n.5) thought the fleet was drawn southward because Columbus used Flemish compasses, biased one point east. In areas of no variation or westerly variation the mariner using one would tend to sail south of a westerly course, or north of an easterly course. Josiah Marvel [personal communication] proposes that Columbus used a Spanish compass calibrated to point north in an area of ½°E magnetic variation (inferred, from Santa Cruz, to be the variation in Palos).

[118] For example, the diagram in Kelley (1987,134).

[119] Really more nearly north of Puerto Rico and the Virgin Islands.

[120] With a compass card divided into 32 points it was impractical to ask the helmsman to keep a course on a fractional point.

[121] Morison (1963,260).

[122] Kelley (1990,29).

[123] See, for example, Gunther (1923,II:163-4) for mid-fifteenth-century drawings of these thirteenth century designs. The *Quadrans vetus* consists of little more than the degree scale along the periphery, a shadow scale boxing the vertex, hour lines, and the signs of the zodiac. The *Quadrans novus* has these same scales, somewhat differently arranged, plus other scales, including the sun's declination, some trigonometric functions, and so forth.

[124] See Jane (1960,73) for a picture of this quadrant design.

[125] Typically these scales are divided into 12ths, 0 corresponding to 0°, 12 to 45°. Examples can be seen in reproductions of Diego Ribero's planisphere of 1529. For example, Nordenskiöld (1897,Pls.XLVIII & XLIX).

[126] Columbus read 100 times the trigonometric tangent of the latitude. The arctangent of 42 hundredths — the number Columbus saw — is about 22°, approximately Columbus's latitude on Cuba.

[127] The earliest English work on the astrolabe, titled *Bread and Milk for Children*, is by Geoffrey Chaucer, written for his 10 year old son, Lewis. Gunther (1923,V:1-132).

[128] Major (1847,128-9).

[129] The rule for correcting the measured altitude of the North Star for its relative position in orbit.

[130] The work was done by Master Rodrigo, a physician, Bishop Ortiz, and José Vizinho, aide to the famous astronomer, Abraham Zacuto of Salamanca. Taylor (1957,162). It was not published until 1509, in manual called *Regiment of the Astrolabe and Quadrant*.

[131] Possibly Mestre Joan Faras, physician and surgeon to D. Manuel, who translated Pomponius Mela's *Geography* into Spanish. See DaCosta (1939,120, n.171) for sources and a good discussion.

[132] Morison (1974,224) puts landfall right at 17°S, off the coast near Monte Pascoal. He moves them north to an anchorage at 16°18' (Porto Seguro), where Mestre Joan and two of the pilots set up their equipment.

[133] Pilot of the *Berrio* during da Gama's voyage.

[134] This large difference may derive from the assumption among Portuguese at the time that there were 16²/₃ leagues per degree of latitude (Bartolomeu Dias was reputed to have verified this), whereas there were really about 18.8 leagues (= 60/3.19). Albuquerque (1963,112,218). In the Cantino world map of 1502, of Portuguese origin, the distance from Lisbon to the most westerly of the Cape Verdes and from thence south to 17°S, is about 59°.7. The difference between the pilots' estimates and Mestre Joan's would be about 124.3 leagues [= 59.7*(18.75 - 16²/₃)]. This lead is not quite the 150 leagues Mestre Joan cites, but it is in the range. The actual course the fleet followed was probably longer than the straight line estimates used here.

[135] This group of stars functioned as a night-time clock, like the Little Dipper.

[136] Presumably Mestre Joan took these altitude readings with a quadrant or astrolabe.

[137] *Las tablas de la India.* The *kamal*, a collection of small rectangular boards, each with a knotted cord attached to its center. The user held the cord in his mouth while holding the board in front of his face, playing out or pulling in the cord until the top and bottom edges of the board lined up with the North Star and the horizon, respectively. The latitude was determined from the number of the knot in the user's teeth.

[138] *Pulgada*, inch, one-twelfth foot. However, the word probably was used in the sense of the knots, or knot numbers, of the *kamal's* cord, not the distance between knots. Because the length of the cord is proportional to the cotangent of half the subtended angle, the knots, to represent equal differences in angle, were probably unevenly distributed along its length as in later *kamals*.

[139] Taylor (1957,129) equates the *pulgada* to 1°36', implying the range of differences of the measurements with the *kamal* was 4°48' to 6°24'. This estimate contrasts with Mestre Joan's claim that his error range at sea was 4° to 5°.

[140] This section draws on James E. Kelley, Jr., "Puzzles the New World Posed for European Mapmakers." *World History Association Conference.* (Philadelphia, 26 June 1992).

[141] Reproduced in Nordenskiöld (1897,Pl.XLIII), and elsewhere.

[142] 20% = 100*([18.8/152/3] - 1). See Kelley (1990,Appendix 4).

[143] For example, Andrés de Morales's chart of Hispaniola of 1509. Alba (1951,Pl.4).

[144] The positioning of the West Indies in *La Cosa* is discussed in Kelley (1990).

[145] The chart of Pedro Reinel, ca.1504 (Kunstmann I, Bayerische Staatsbibliothek, Munich), establishes the magnetic variation for the Newfoundland area. See Winter (1937). Kelley (1990) estimates 13°W for the central Bahamas assuming an unbiased compass was used to orient the islands. For a compass biased ½-point east, the more probable case, the estimate reduces to about 7°W.

[146] The true bearing of Savannah to northern Nova Scotia is about 50°.

[147] Hispanic Society of America, New York. Reproduced in Cumming, et al (1972,Pl.87).

[148] Royal 20.E.IX, f.23v,24r, British Library. Prepared for Henry VIII. Reproduced in Cumming, et al (1972,Pl.116).

[149] Biblioteca Apostolica Vaticana, Vatican City. Reproduced in Almagià (1944,I:Pl.24).

[150] Casteñada, et al (1983).

[151] Lamb (1969,52-3).

[152] Alba (1951,Pl.17). In his *Book of Longitudes* Santa Cruz takes up the issue of the "high" latitudes of contemporary Spanish charts.

[153] See the discussion in Kelley (1990,34-5).

Reference List

Alba, Duque de, and others. *Mapas españoles de America siglos XV-XVII*. Madrid: Real Academia de la Historica, 1951.

Albertis, Eurico Alberto d'. "Le Construzioni navale e l'arte della Navigazione al tempo di Cristofero Colombo." In *Raccolta Colombiana*. Rome, 1893, Pt. IV, Vol. I, 185-91.

Albuquerque, Luís Mendonça de. *O Livro de Marinharia de André Pires*. Lisbon: Junta de Investigaçoes do Ultramar, 1963.

Almagià, Roberto, ed. *Planisferi Carte Nautiche e Affini dal Secolo XIV al XVII* esistenti nella Biblioteca Apostolica Vaticana. Vol. I of *Monumenta Cartographica Vaticana*. Vatican City: Biblioteca Apostolica Vaticana, 1944.

Balmer, R.T. "The Operation of Sand Clocks and their Medieval Development." *Technology and Culture* 19 (1978), 615-32.

Bensaude, Joaquim. *L'Astronomie Nautique au Portugal a l'époque des Grandes Découvertes*. Berne: Paul Haupt Verlag, 1912. Rpr. Amsterdam: N. Israel/Meridian Publishing, 1967.

Bowie, Theodore. *The Sketchbook of Villard de Honnecourt*. Bloomington: Indiana Univ. Press, 1959.

Burwash, Dorothy. *English Merchant Shipping 1460-1540*. Toronto: Univ. of Toronto Press, 1947.

Campbell, Tony. "Portolan Charts from the Late Thirteenth Century to 1500." In *Cartography in Prehistoric, Ancient, and Medieval Europe and the Mediterranean 371-463*. Vol. I of *The History of Cartography*. Eds. J.B. Harley and David Woodward. Chicago & London: Univ. of Chicago Press, 1987.

Carus-Wilson, E.M. *The Overseas Trade of Bristol in the Later Middle Ages*. Bristol: Bristol Record Society, 1937.

Carus-Wilson, E.M. *Medieval Merchant Venturers*. London: Methuen, 1954.

Casteñada Delgado, Paulino, Mariano Cuesta, and Pilar Hernández Aparicio. *Alonso de Chaves: Quatri partitu en cosmografia practica, y por otro nombre espejo de navegantes*. Madrid: Instituto de Historia y Cultura Naval, 1983.

Cerezo Martinez, Ricardo. "La derrota del primer viaje de Colón." *Revista de Historia Naval* 18 (1987), 5-13.

Chardon, Roland. "The Linear League in North America." *Annals of the Association of American Geographers* 70 (1960), 129-53.

Charlier, Georges A. "Value of the Mile Used at Sea by Cristobal Colon During *His First Voyage,*" *Proceedings First San Salvador Conference: Columbus And His World.* Compiled by Donald T. Gerace. Fort Lauderdale, FL: CCFL Bahamian Field Station, 1987, 121-40.

Charlier, Georges A. *Etude complete de la navigation et de l'itinéraire de Cristobal Colon lors de son voyage de découverte de l'Amérique.* Liège, Belgique: "Le Closérie," 1988

Cotrugli, Benedetto. *De navigatione liber.* Taylor MSS 557, pre-1600 series, Yale. Italy, 1464.

Cumming, W.P., R.A. Skelton and D.B. Quinn. *The Discovery of North America.* New York: American Heritage Press, 1972.

DaCosta, A. Fontoura. *A Marinharia dos Descobrimentos.* Lisboa: Agencia Geral das Colonias, 1939.

Denoix, Commandant. "Les Problèmes de Navigation au Début des Grandes Découvertes." In Mollat (1960, 131-142).

Dunn, Oliver C. and James E. Kelley, Jr. 1989. *The Diario of Christopher Columbus' First Voyage to America 1492-1493.* Norman, OK: Oklahoma Univ. Press, 1989.

Fantoni, Girolamo, and Mario Ingravalle. "Alla ricerca della lega di Cristoforo Colombo." *Revista Marittima* 361 (1987), 65-89.

Fell, Barry. "Ancient Iberian Magnetic Compass Dials from Liria, Spain." *Occasional Publications of the Epigraphic Society* 3 (September, 1976), art. 57.

Ferro, Gaetano. "Columbus and his Sailings, According to the 'Diary' of the First Voyage: Observations of a Geographer." In Gerace (1987), 99-114.

Fox, Gustavus V. "An Attempt to Solve the Problem of the First Landing Place of Columbus in the New World," *Report of the Superintendent of the U.S. Coast and Geodetic Survey for 1880, Appendix 18,* Washington: Government Printing Office, 1882, 346-411.

Franco, Salvador García. *La Legua Nautica en la Edad Media.* Madrid: Instituto Histórico de Marina, 1957.

Fuson, Robert H., and Walter H. Treftz. "A Theoretical Reconstruction of the First Atlantic Crossing of Christopher Columbus." *Proceedings of the Association of American Geographers* 8 (1976), 155-59.

Gelcich, Eugen. 1885. "Beiträge zur Geschichte des Zeitalters der Entdeckungen. I. Columbus als Nautiker und als Seemann." *Zeitschrift der Gesellschaft für Erdkunde zu Berlin* 20 (1885), 280-324.

Gerace, Donald T., ed. *Proceedings First San Salvador Conference: Columbus and His World.* Fort Lauderdale, FL: CCFL Bahamian Field Station, 1987.

Goldsmith, R.A., and P.L. Richardson. *Reconstructing Columbus's First Transatlantic Track and Landfall Using Climatological Winds and Currents.* Technical Report WHOI-87-46. Woods Hole, MA: Woods Hole Oceanographic Institution, November 1987.

Goldsmith, R.A., and P.L. Richardson. *Numerical Simulations of Columbus' Atlantic Crossings.* Woods Hole, MA.: Woods Hole Oceanographic Institution, 9 November 1990)

Gunther, R.T. *Astronomy.* Vol II of *Early Science in Oxford.* Rpr. London: Dawsons of Pall Mall, 1967.

Gunther, R.T. *Chaucer and Messahalla on the Astrolabe.* Vol V of *Early Science in Oxford.* Rpr. London: Dawsons of Pall Mall, 1967.

Harrisse, Henry. *The Discovery of North America: A Critical, Documentary, and Historic Investigation, and so forth.* London and Paris, 1892. Rpr. Amsterdam: N. Israel, 1969.

Herrera y Tordesillas, Antonio de. *Descripcion de las islas, Tierra Firme del mar oceano, que llaman Indias Ocidentales.* Madrid: Juan Flamenco, 1601.

Hewson, J.B. *A History of the Practice of Navigation.* Glasgow: Brown, Son & Ferguson, 1951. Revised 1963.

Hinz, Walther. *Islamische Masse und Gewichte*. Leiden: E.J. Brill, 1955.

Jados, Stanley S. *Consulate of the Sea and Related Documents*. University: Univ. of Alabama Press, 1975.

Jane, Cecil. *The Journal of Christopher Columbus*. Rev. and annotated by L.A. Vigneras, with appendix by R.A. Skelton. New York: Potter, 1960.

Jane, Cecil, trans. and ed. *The Four Voyages of Columbus*. New York: Dover, 1988. Slightly altered and corrected reprint in one volume of The Hakluyt Society Second Series, Nos. LXV and LXX, published in 1930 and 1933, respectively.

Judge, Joseph. "A Note on the 2.82-Nautical-Mile League." A Columbus Casebook: Supplement to "Where Columbus Found the New World." *National Geographic Magazine* Nov. (1986), 59

Kelley, James E., Jr. "The Oldest Portolan Chart in the New World." *Terrae Incognitae* 9 (1977), 22-48.

Kelley, James E., Jr. *Charms, Starsigns and Weather Lore in Defense against the Storm*. Melrose Park, PA, 1977. Presented to the Society for the History of Discoveries, Tucson meeting, Oct. 27-29, 1977.

Kelley, James E., Jr. "Non-Mediterranean Influences that Shaped the Atlantic in the Early Portolan Charts." *Imago Mundi* 31 (1979), 18-35.

Kelley, James E., Jr. "In the Wake of Columbus on the Portolan Chart." *Terrae Incognitae* 15 (1983), 77-111.

Kelley, James E., Jr. 1987. "The Navigation of Columbus on His First Voyage to America" In Gerace (1987,121-140).

Kelley, James E., Jr. "The Map of the Bahamas implied by Chaves's *Derrotero*: What is its Relevance to the First Landfall Question?" *Imago Mundi* 42 (1990), 26-49.

Kelley, James E., Jr. "James E. Kelley Jr. Expatiates on the Leeway Issue." *Encounter '92* 5, No. 1, (March 1991), 15-16.

Kelley, James E., Jr. "How Did Columbus Estimate Speed at Sea?" *Encounter'92* 5, No. 2, (October 1991), 7-9.

Kelley, James E., Jr. "Juan Ponce de Leon's Discovery of Florida: Herrera's Narrative revisited." *Revista de Historia de América* 111 (1992), 31-65.

Knox-Johnston, Robin. "In the Wake of Columbus." *The Journal of Navigation* 45, No. 1, (1992), 1-11.

Kraus, H.P., Booksellers. *Twenty-five Manuscripts. Catalog 95.* New York: H.P. Kraus, ca. 1961.

Kretschmer, Konrad. *Die italienischen Portolane des Mittelalters: Ein Beitrag zur Geschichte der Kartographie und Nautik, mit einer Kartenbeilage.* Berlin: E.S. Mittler und Sohn, 1909. Rpr. Hildesheim: Georg Olms, 1962.

Kreutz, Barbara M. "Mediterranean Contributions to the Medieval Mariner's Compass." *Technology and Culture* 14 (1973), 367-83.

Lamb, Ursula. "Science by Litigation: A Cosmographic Feud." *Terrae Incognitae* 1 (1969), 40-57.

Lane, Fredrick C. "The Economic Meaning of the Invention of the Compass." *American Historical Review* 67 (1963), 605-17.

Latham, R.E. *Revised Medieval Latin Word-list from British and Irish Sources.* London: Oxford Univ. Press, 1965.

Lelewel, Joachim. *Géographie du Moyen âge.* 5 vols. Bruxelles: Chez V^e et J. Philliet, 1852.

Machabey, Armand. *La Métrologie dans les musées de province et sa contribution á l'histoire des poids et mesures en France depuis le treizième siècle.* Paris: Centre National de la Recherche Scientifique, 1962.

Mallett, Michael E. *The Florentine Galleys in the Fifteenth Century.* Oxford: Clarendon Press, 1967.

Magnaghi, Alberto. "I presunti errori che vengono attribuiti a Colombo nella determinazione della latitudini." *Bolletino società geo grafica italiana,* 16th series, 5 (1928), 459-94, 553-82.

Major, R.H., trans. and ed. *Select Letters of Christopher Columbus with Other Original Documents Relating to His Four Voyages to the New World.* London: Hakluyt Society, 1847.

Marcus, G.J. "The Navigation of the Norsemen." *The Mariner's Mirror* 39 (1953), 112-31.

Marden, Luis. "Tracking Columbus Across the Atlantic." *National Geographic Magazine* 170, No. 5, (Nov. 1986), 572-577.

Markham, Clements. *The Journal of Christopher Columbus (During his First Voyage, 1492-93) and Documents Relating to the Voyages of John Cabot and Gaspar Corte Real.* London: Hakluyt Society, 1893.

McElroy, John W. "The Ocean Navigation of Columbus on his First Voyage." *The American Neptune* 1 (1941), 209-40.

Mollat, Michel, et al. *Le Navire et l'Economie Maritime du Nord de l'Europe du Moyen-Age au XVIIe Siecle.* Paris: S.E.V.P.E.N., 1960.

Morison, S.E. "Columbus and Polaris." *The American Neptune* 1 (1941), 1-20, 123-37.

Morison, S.E. *Admiral of the Ocean Sea: A Life of Christopher Columbus.* 2 Vols. Boston: Little, Brown, 1942.

Morison, S.E., ed. and trans. *Journals and Other Documents on the Life and Voyages of Christopher Columbus.* New York: Heritage, 1963.

Morison, S.E. *The European Discovery of America: The Southern Voyages, A.D. 1492-1616.* New York: Oxford Univ. Press, 1974.

Nansen, Fridtjof. *In Northern Mists: Arctic Explorations in Early Times.* Trans. Arthur G. Chater. 2 Vols. New York: Frederick A. Stokes Company, 1911.

Nordenskiöld, A.E. *Periplus: An Essay on the Early History of Charts and Sailing-Directions.* Trans. Francis A. Bather. Stockholm 1897. Rpr. New York: Burt Franklin.

Nunn, George E. *The Geographical Conceptions of Columbus.* New York: American Geographical Society, 1924.

Obregón, Mauricio. *La Primera Vuelta al Mundo: Magallanes, Elcano y El Libro Perdido de la Nao Victoria.* Bogotá: Plaza & Janes, 1984.

Peck, Douglas T. *An Empirical Reconstruction of Columbus' Discovery Voyage in 1492 and his Return Voyage in 1493.* Bradenton, FL, December, 1991. Submitted for publication.

Raccolta di documenti e studi pubblicati dalla R. Commissione Colombiana, pel quarto centenario dalla scoperta dell'America. Cesare de Lollis, ed. 14 Vols. Rome: Ministero della pubblica istruzione, 1892-94.

Ravenstein, E.G. *Martin Behaim His Life and His Globe.* London: George Philip & Son, 1908.

Richardson, Philip L., and Roger A. Goldsmith. "The Columbus Land-fall: Voyage Track Corrected for Winds and Currents." *Oceanus* 30, No. 3, (1987), 3-10.

Schott, Charles A. "An Inquiry into the Variation of the Compass off the Bahama Islands, at the Time of the Landfall of Columbus in 1492," *Report of the Superintendent of the U.S. Coast and Geodetic Survey for 1880, Appendix 19.* Washington: Government Printing Office, 1882), 412-17.

Sidders, Juan Carlos. "Los viajes de Colón y las nuevas investigacions realizadas por la National Geographic Society." *Revista de Historia Naval* 5 (1987), 7-13.

Skelton, R.A. *Explorers' Maps.* London: Routledge & Kegan Paul, 1958.

Smith, John. *A Sea Grammar* [of 1627]. Ed. Kermit Goell. London: Printed by Michael Joseph. 1970.

Steger, Ernst. "Untersuchen uber italienische Seekarten des Mittelalters auf Grund der cartometrischen Methode." Dissertation, Göttingen, 1896.

Strachan, Michal, and Boies Penrose, eds. *The East India Company Journals of Captain William Keeling and Master Thomas Bonner, 1615-1617.* Minneapolis: Univ. of Minnesota Press, 1971.

Taylor, E.G.R. *The Haven-Finding Art.* New York: Abelard-Schuman, 1957.

Taylor, E.G.R., ed. *A Regiment for the Sea and Other Writings on Navigation by William Bourne of Gravesend, a Gunner (c.1535-1582).* Cambridge, England: Published for the Hakluyt Society at the Univ. Press, 1963.

Thacher, John B., ed. *Christopher Columbus: His Life, His Work, His Remains, as Revealed by Original Printed and Manuscript Records, Together with an Essay of Peter Martyr Anghera and Bartolomé de las Casas, the first Historians of America.* 3 Vols. New York: G.P. Putnam's Sons, 1903-04.

Uzielli, G. and P. Amat di S. Filippo, eds. *Mappamondi Carte Nautiche, Portolani. Ed altri Monumenti Cartografici Specialmente Italiani dei Secoli XIII-XVII.* 2nd. ed. Rome, 1882. Rpr. Amsterdam: Meridian Publishing Company, 1967.

Van Bemmelen, W. *Die Abweichung der Magnetnadel: Observations of the Royal Magnetical and Meteorological Observatory at Batavia* 21 (1899).

Velasco, Juan López de. *Geografía y Descripción Universal de las Indias.* Ed. Marcos Jiménez de la Espada; Preliminary study by: María del Carmen González Muñoz. *Biblioteca de Autores Espanoles, tomo CCXLVIII.* Madrid: Ediciones Atlas, 1971.

Vignaud, H. *Toscanelli and Columbus: The Letter and Chart of Toscanelli.* London: Sands & Co., 1902.

Wagner, Hermann. "The Origin of the Medieval Italian Nautical Charts." *Report of the Sixth International Geographical Congress.* London, 1895, 695-702.

Wagner, Hermann. "Der Ursprung de 'kleinen Seemeile' auf den mittelalterlichen Seekarten der Italiener." *Kögnigliche Gesellschaft der Wissenschaft der Philologische-historische Klasse 1900* 3 (1900), 271-85.

Waters, D.W. "Early Time and Distance Measurement at Sea." *Journal of the Institute of Navigation* 8 (1955), 153-173.

Waters, D.W. *The Art of Navigation in England in Elizabethan and Early Stuart Times.* New Haven: Yale Univ. Press, 1958.

Waters, D.W. *The Rutters of the Sea: The Sailing Directions of Pierre Garcie.* New Haven: Yale Univ. Press, 1967.

Winter, Heinrich. "The Pseudo-Labrador and the Oblique Meridian." *Imago Mundi* 2 (1937), 61-73.

Winter, Heinrich. "The True Position of Hermann Wagner in the Controversy of the Compass Chart." *Imago Mundi* 5 (1948), 21-26.

Zupko, Ronald Edward. *French Weights and Measures before the Revolution.* Bloomington & London: Indiana Univ. Press, 1978.

IV

Aftermath of the Voyage

The Medieval Church-State Conflict

in the New World

James M. Muldoon

Some time ago, Professor Brian Tierney gave a plenary address at the Patristic-Medieval-Renaissance Conference in which he criticized the failure of historians of political thought to appreciate the medieval underpinnings of early modern political thought. The recently-published work of Quentin Skinner was the most obvious object of Tierney's criticism, but Skinner is not the only historian of early modern Europe who can be criticized for such a failure. In a series of subsequent articles, Tierney has continued to criticize other historians and political scientists for failing to appreciate the sophistication of medieval political thought and the role it played in shaping the political discourse of the early modern era. [1] Most recently, Tierney has observed that "[m]edievalists sometimes complain that their work is 'marginalized,' not sufficiently regarded by scholars working in other fields of research." At the same time, he pointed out that the fault does not rest entirely with non-medievalists. In the scholarly area that interests him, for example, Tierney concluded that with regard to "the history of natural-rights theories, perhaps it is we medievalists who are at fault." [2]

In one sense, Tierney is fighting a battle that has gone on since the fifteenth century when phrases such as the Dark Ages and the Gothic Age became the standard judgment on the Middle Ages. Renaissance humanists had condemned medieval art as the barbarous production of a decadent era, and Protestant Reformers described medieval religion as so deeply sunk in error as to require divine intervention in order to rescue mankind from the clutches of the Church of Rome. [3] This view of the Middle Ages received its canonical statement in Gibbon's *Decline and Fall*. At the end of the twentieth century, as we enter what some observers have labelled the post-Enlightenment period of history, we should emend the Renaissance-Enlightenment view of the Middle Ages and begin to see the medieval period on its own terms. Such a hope is, however, likely to be frustrated because of the innate conservatism of the college and university curriculum, reinforced by a long-standing prejudice against the Middle Ages.

The quincentennial celebration of Columbus's first voyage could provide an opportunity for medievalists and early modernists to come together in a common project to further our understanding of one of the truly great moments in world history, the European discovery of the Americas. [4] After all, it is quite clear that Columbus was not resolutely turning his back on the experience of medieval Europe when he set sail in 1492, even if Washington Irving had said that he did. That is, while the scene of Columbus demonstrating that the world is round to a committee of scholastic philosophers and theologians who believed otherwise makes for good theater and reinforces prejudices about the Middle Ages, it is, of course, wrong. At the very least, Columbus built upon almost a century of Portuguese and Castilian maritime and colonizing activity in the Atlantic. Historians of technology have traced the medieval development of maps and maritime technology that shaped Columbus's outlook, and students of colonialism have found the medieval roots of colonial practices. Intellectual historians have demonstrated that the official documents that demarcate stages of the age of expansion have deep roots in the medieval experience. [5] It is even possible to argue that Columbus's career marked the beginning of the second phase of European expansion, the first phase being a movement that had begun about the middle of the tenth century as the fundamental elements of European culture moved out from the European heartland, the old Carolingian empire. [6] Until at least the mid-fourteenth century, Europe had an expanding frontier, and Europeans developed the institutions and attitudes characteristic of frontier societies, attitudes that shaped the outlook of Columbus and his successors and the institutions that they employed as they established colonial societies along the new and expanding frontier. [7]

And yet, even though medievalists are well aware of the medieval substructure of the great age of European expansion, they have not been able to convey the significance of this material to specialists in the history of post-1492 expansion. Part of the reason for this may be that the fifteenth century is a kind of academic no-man's land, the point at which the Middle Ages begin to fade and the modern world has not yet come into focus. It is a period that forms a great divide rather than a link between the medieval and the modern worlds. Thus it is easy for early modernists to admit some medieval roots of European overseas expansion, but then to focus their attention on the period after 1492. For example, many of the general histories of expansion trace European expansion back to the early fifteenth century, to the Portuguese capture of Ceuta in 1415, an understandable beginning but somewhat misleading. [8] Indeed, it might be argued that the fifteenth-century contribution to European expansion was in fact less significant than the contribution of earlier periods.

One way to demonstrate the importance of the medieval experience in the age of overseas expansion is to consider the relationship between two significant moments in European intellectual history. The first is the medieval church-state conflict; the second is the debate about the rights of the inhabitants of the Americas that was at the center of Spanish intellectual life in the sixteenth and seventeenth centuries. At first glance these moments in intellectual history would seem to have little connection. After all, there was no church-state conflict in the New World because Ferdinand, Isabella, and Charles V had obtained complete administrative control of the church in the Spanish world from the papacy. The patronate that the Spanish monarchs possessed eliminated the most important traditional sources of conflict between the spiritual and the temporal powers. As C.R. Boxer pointed out, the Castilian monarchs, and their Portuguese counterparts, obtained the right to establish every kind of ecclesiastical structure, from parish churches to cathedrals, to nominate candidates for all ecclesiastical offices within their sphere of jurisdiction, "to administer ecclesiastical jurisdictions and revenues, and to veto papal Bulls and Briefs which were not first cleared through the respective crown chancery." The consequence of these rights was that "in practice every missionary prelate and priest . . . could only take up his appointment with the approval of the Crown concerned; and he depended on that Crown for his financial support." [9] As a result, there never existed in the Spanish empire the kind of conflict that characterized the relationship between medieval popes and German emperors or English kings. At least structurally, the relationship between Spanish monarchs and the papacy was a carefully worked out balance of interests that gave the monarchs a free hand in administering the institutional structure of the church within Spain in return for advancing Rome's spiritual goals.

If there was no conflict between kings and popes in the sixteenth-century Spanish world, then how can it be said that the medieval church-state conflict had a significant role to play in the Spanish overseas empire? When Spanish intellectuals began to debate the legitimacy of the conquest of the New World in the early sixteenth century, they debated it in terms derived from the canon lawyers of the twelfth and thirteenth centuries. This perhaps startling observation in fact is the observation of Garrett Mattingly, made many years ago in his classic work *Renaissance Diplomacy*. [10] Mattingly argued that the fundamental ideas of the sixteenth-century Spanish writers on the conquest of the Americas came from Thomas Aquinas and from "the twelfth-century canonists with explicit elaborations in the fourteenth and fifteenth centuries. . . ." [11] Mattingly based this conclusion on the work of James Brown Scott, a lawyer and advocate for world peace through world law in the early twentieth century. [12] What Mattingly did not appreciate was that, while Scott's discussion of the Spanish writers on international law was on the right track, there were significant flaws in it as well. Mattingly after all was a Renaissance historian, not a medievalist, and as such had to rely on what appeared to be the best available material on the roots of international law.

Why did the Spanish writers of the sixteenth century, facing the moral and legal problems that the discovery of the Americas posed, rely on medieval thinkers to provide an intellectual basis for their discussions? Where else would they look? When Europeans approached the New World, they did so with a body of ideas inherited from ancient and medieval texts that appeared capable of being stretched and extended to comprehend the new worlds that were opening up to Europeans. As Anthony Grafton has pointed out, "the actual pace of change was slower and the power of inherited authority more durable and more complex than many historians have acknowledged." [13] In intellectual matters, as in technology, the sixteenth century was quite conservative. If Columbus could identify the shorelines of the islands that he encountered in the Caribbean with the coastlines indicated on the maps of Asia at his disposal, why expect that intellectuals who had at their disposal intellectual road maps about the political order should do otherwise? As V. Flint has pointed out, "Columbus's picture of the east was built of layer upon layer of medieval mental geology." [14] The same geological strata underlay the outlook of the academics, lawyers, and bureaucrats who debated the legitimacy of the conquest of the Americas. To understand how and why these Spanish thinkers dealt with the moral and legal problems raised by discovery of the Americas, we must take up an intellectual geologist's hammer, crack open these underlying strata, and reveal the mental world contained therein.

This debate was the only time in the history of expansion and conquest that a conquering nation publicly debated the legitimacy of its actions and sought legal and moral justification for them. In other words, the debate was so novel and unique that it could have had only the most fragile roots in the Middle Ages. Thus, it is possible to discuss the medieval origins of this debate and then to move on quickly to the sixteenth-century development of the ideas involved. For example, some fifty years ago, J.H. Parry wrote an interesting book entitled *The Spanish Theory of Empire in the Sixteenth Century*. He traced the arguments about the extent of papal jurisdiction over infidels that lay at the heart of the debate about the legitimacy of the conquest to the writings of the canonist Hostiensis (d. 1270). [15] To that extent, he was more familiar with medieval sources than Mattingly who wrote after him. Parry appears to have assumed, however, that Hostiensis was the only medieval canonist who discussed the relationship between the papacy and the infidels. As a result, he was able to make a sharp contrast between Hostiensis's views and those of sixteenth-century writers. According to Parry,

> The doctrine of universal papal dominion, in temporal as in spiritual matters, usually associated with the name of Henry of Susa (Ostiensis), was, it is true, well known to canonists in the fifteenth and early sixteenth centuries, but was certainly not universally accepted. It was a relic of the medieval conception of the word, as a homogeneous Christendom with an infidel fringe.

Parry then contrasted Hostiensis's views with those of many "sixteenth-century jurists, in Spain as elsewhere, [who] rejected the Ostiensian doctrine. . . ." [16]

In so stating his opinion, Parry sharply distinguished between the medieval position on Christian relations with non-Christian societies and the sixteenth-century one. He argued that sixteenth-century Spanish thinkers judged Hostiensis's opinion "not only . . . theologically unsound but . . . unrealistic" as well. [17] Phrased this way, Hostiensis's argument typified medieval thinking, that is "unrealistic" thought about social and political issues, while sixteenth-century Spanish thinkers, the advance guard of modernity, were clearly more realistic and, by implication, more modern. The result would logically be that medieval thought on such issues would be of little interest to students of the early modern era because sixteenth-century writers had rejected it.

There are, however, three major flaws in Parry's argument. In the first place, the medieval canonists did not assume that the world was "a homogeneous Christendom with an infidel fringe" as Parry would have us believe. The canonists recognized the presence of Muslim and Jewish communities within Europe and devoted one title of the *Decretales* (bk. 5, tit. 6) to issues arising from their presence. [18] It is true that the canonists would have preferred an entirely Christian world, but they knew the realities of medieval Europe quite well. In the second place, Hostiensis's opinion on papal jurisdiction was not the only nor even the dominant treatment of papal jurisdiction within the canon law tradition. Hostiensis had offered this opinion in response to the opinion of his master, Pope Innocent IV (1243-1254) in a commentary on the decretal *Quod super his* (X.3.34.8). [19] Innocent IV had presented a more nuanced theory of papal jurisdiction than had Hostiensis. Where Hostiensis argued that with the coming of Christ all non-Christians lost any claim to *dominium*, that is to legitimate possession of self-government and property because, in the final analysis, *dominium* rested on grace after the Incarnation, Innocent IV argued that all men, regardless of their spiritual condition, possessed *dominium* and the pope could not arbitrarily deprive them of it.

The second flaw in Parry's argument lies in his discussion of the sixteenth-century Spanish thinkers who developed the debate about the rights of the peoples of the New World. In discussing the work of Francis Vitoria (1480?-1546), the Dominican theologian whose *De Indis* provided the first extended treatment of the legitimacy of the conquest of the Americas, Parry asserted that Vitoria "was probably the first serious writer to reject firmly and unequivocally all claim of Pope or Emperor to exercise temporal jurisdiction over other princes." [20] Apparently, Parry was unaware of Marsilio of Padua and other medieval critics of papal power. [21] He obviously had not read Innocent IV's opinion either and, furthermore, he had not read Vitoria very closely. Vitoria did not "unequivocally" reject all papal claims to temporal jurisdiction over secular rulers. Among the lawful titles that the Spanish might assert to claim possession of the Americas, Vitoria listed the following:

> 10. The Pope could entrust to the Spaniards alone the task of converting the Indian aborigines and could forbid to all others not only preaching, but trade too, if the propagation of Christianity would thus be furthered.
> 12. How the aborigines who hinder the spread of the Gospel ... may be coerced by the Spaniards, so long as no scandal is caused. ...
> 14. The Indians might have come under the sway of the Spaniards by the fact that, after the conversion of a large part of them to Christianity, the Pope, either with or without a request on their part, might on reasonable grounds have given them a Christian prince, such as the King of Spain, and driven out their infidel lords. [22]

Furthermore, not only did Vitoria not "unequivocally" reject papal claims to jurisdiction over secular rulers, even his carefully nuanced discussion of the nature and extent of papal jurisdiction over infidel rulers was not original with him. Careful analysis of the structure of his *De Indis*, the lectures in which he discussed the legitimate and the illegitimate titles that the Spanish could allege to justify their possession of the Americas, makes it quite clear that Vitoria based his opinion largely on the commentary of Innocent IV on the decretal *Quod super his*. [23] In other words, when Vitoria sought to comprehend the moral, philosophical, and theological issues associated with the conquest of the New World, he did not create new terminology and new categories. Rather, he took the language and categories of the thirteenth-century canonists and applied them to the situation with which he was dealing.

Throughout the course of the debate about the legitimacy of the conquest, Spanish intellectuals continued to base their discussion of the legitimacy of the conquest on the legal commentaries from the thirteenth century. In particular, the commentaries of Innocent IV and Hostiensis remained the basis for all subsequent discussion of the legitimacy of the conquest. This is true even of the most famous of all sixteenth-century debates about the legitimacy of the conquest of the New World, the confrontation between Bartolomé de las Casas (1474-1566) and Juan Ginés de Sepúlveda (1490-1573) before an imperial commission at Valladolid in 1550. [24] It is, of course, possible to see this debate in simplistic terms as the confrontation between the passionate Las Casas, associate of the Columbus family and early colonist in the New World, a man who underwent a spiritual conversion and turned his formidable energies to the defense of the Indians whom he had once been willing to enslave and Sepúlveda, the cool and detached humanist who argued that the Indians were, in Aristotle's terms, natural slaves who should be ruled by the Spanish for their own good. The consequence is to see Las Casas and Sepúlveda as representing two distinct intellectual traditions with regard to the Spanish role in the Americas. Parry, for example, sums up their differences this way:

> Sepúlveda and Las Casas, whatever the original springs of their thought, represented the two divergent yet complementary tendencies of the imperialist theory of their time. Both sought to modify royal policy and to limit the exercise of the royal will. The thought of both was firmly rooted in the Middle Ages. [25]

Here again, Parry recognizes the medieval roots of sixteenth-century Spanish thought but fails to appreciate the true nature and extent of those roots. In fact, the differences between Las Casas and Sepúlveda reduced themselves in the final analysis to whether or not the peoples of the New World could be best brought to baptism and placed under Christian rulers peacefully, as Las Casas argued, or whether force would first be required to pacify and civilize them before being baptized, as Sepúlveda argued. Both writers supported their arguments with materials found in Gratian's *Decretum* as well as with a number of decretals dealing with the just war, with the relationship of conquest to baptism, and with the extent of papal jurisdiction. The "original springs of their thought" in other words turn out to be the *Decretum* and the *Decretales*, the basic volumes of the canon law. [26] What was not debated by Las Casas and Sepúlveda was the extent of papal jurisdiction. Both recognized the responsibility of the pope to seek the salvation of all men. They differed on the most suitable means for achieving that end.

Why did the Spanish monarchs reject Sepúlveda's argument about the naturally servile status of the Indians. It would have been a useful argument for an expanding empire interested in defending its conquests. Inasmuch as Sepúlveda was also one of the most prominent humanists in Spain, one might have thought that this argument would have been seen as an up-to-date intellectual defense of Spanish policy, one acceptable to the humanistically-trained bureaucrats who advised Charles V. The usual explanation for the Spanish monarch's rejection of the Aristotelian argument about the naturally servile status of barbarous peoples such as the inhabitants of the Americas is that, if accepted, the Spanish settlers who had enslaved Indians would be well on the way to creating a feudal society in the Americas of the sort that the centralizing monarchs of sixteenth-century Spain were eliminating at home. [27] That is no doubt true to some extent.

There was another reason, however, for rejecting Sepúlveda's argument as a basis for the Spanish conquest of the Americas. If the Spanish rested their claim to the Americas on the Aristotelian notion that the Indians were naturally servile people, they would have lost any basis for asserting a monopoly of contact with the peoples of the New World. The Aristotelian argument would authorize the leader of any superior society, meaning any European Christian ruler, to invade the Americas and subdue the people found there. The only way for the Spanish to guarantee their monopoly was to base possession of the Americas on papal grant. Thus the Spanish rested their possession of the New World on the bulls issued by Pope Alexander VI (1492-1503) for the purpose of securing the conversion of the inhabitants of the Americas to Christianity. [28] The assumption was that the Indians were rational human beings capable of understanding and accepting Christian teachings. It was on that basis that Alexander VI gave to the Castilian monarchs the right to occupy the Americas. If the Indians were truly natural slaves because of their inferior mental capacity, presumably they could not become Christians. If that were the case, then the pope would have had no basis for authorizing the Spanish conquest of the New World, because his jurisdiction extended only to those with rational souls.

Thus, the debate about the legitimacy of the conquest of the Americas, the debate about the rationality of the inhabitants of the Americas, the debate about the rights of the Indians, were all subordinate to the old medieval debate about the nature and extent of papal jurisdiction in spirituals and in temporals. If the pope did not have the authority to grant the Spanish monarchs a monopoly of contact with the Americas, then Spanish claim to America failed. Consequently the Spanish writers of the sixteenth century invariably defended universal papal jurisdiction in spiritual matters and the consequences of that jurisdiction in temporal matters as well.

The extent to which Spanish writers were willing to go in defending papal power reached a peak in the seventeenth century when one legal writer invoked Boniface VIII's (1294-1303) *Unam sanctam* as part of the defense of Spanish claims in the Americas. The writer was not, as one might expect, some extreme papalist but a high-ranking Spanish official, Juan de Solórzano Pereira (1575-1654), who had served as a judge in Lima and then returned to Spain where he served on the Council of Castile and the Council of the Indies. His *De Indiarum iure* was probably the longest and most thoroughly developed defense of the Spanish conquest of the Americas ever written. His defense of the conquest rested on the right of Alexander VI to grant the Americas to the Spanish on the terms outlined in *Inter caetera*. After discussing nine traditional arguments supporting the conquest only to reject them, Solórzano moved to what he termed "The tenth and most efficacious title [to possession of the Americas], that which is derived from the grant and gift of the Roman Pontiff. . . ." [29] It is in this section of the work that Solórzano included the bulk of the text of *Unam sanctam*. [30] Solórzano placed Boniface's famous bull at the end of a subsection of a chapter dealing with papal power. In his opinion, a good Catholic would have to accept the outline of papal power contained in this document. His emphasis, however, was not on papal power alone but on the co-operation between the two powers that the bull described. Keeping to the mainstream of medieval thought on Canon Law concerning the right relationship between the two powers, spiritual and temporal, he argued that the secular ruler, acting at the request of the pope, undertakes a particular task, in this case the conversion of the peoples of the New World.

Solórzano buttressed his argument about papal power by citing a number of situations in which secular rulers had undertaken spiritual tasks at the request of the papacy and, as a reward for their efforts, acquired control of new lands. The most interesting of the examples that he gave concerned the bull *Laudabiliter* that Pope Adrian IV (1154-1159) issued to Henry II (1154-1189). The bull authorized Henry II to enter Ireland in order to bring the people back to the proper observance of the Faith. To achieve this spiritual goal, the English were authorized to take control of the entire island and retained possession even after Henry VIII (1509-1547) and the Reformation Parliament rejected papal authority. Thus, in Solórzano's opinion, if the current English monarch, Charles I (1625-1649), denied the pope's power to grant the Americas to the Spanish, then, logically, the English would have to surrender Ireland since they held it on exactly the same basis as the Spanish held the Americas. [31] Clearly Solórzano did not believe that Charles I would surrender Ireland, but he certainly did believe that the historical record of papal-royal relations demonstrated the right of the pope to subject people to Christian rulers for their own spiritual good.

In effect, as Solórzano's arguments demonstrate, the legitimacy of the Spanish conquest of the Americas depended upon accepting a particular theory of papal power and jurisdiction that the canon lawyers had developed centuries earlier. One could argue, quite cynically, that the Spanish monarchs and their advisors simply "theory shopped" until they found a legal theory that would justify the Spanish monopoly in the Americas, just as twentieth-century American lawyers "judge shop" in order to find a judge likely to be sympathetic to their cause. In the Spanish case, however, it was not necessary to look very far for a theory of papal power that would justify Spanish activities, a theory that would satisfy both Spanish and papal interests.

The legitimacy of the Spanish conquest of the New World rested on the dualist theory of power that the twelfth-and thirteenth-century canonists had developed. This theory assumed that popes and secular rulers had autonomous spheres of jurisdiction and neither could interfere in the other's jurisdiction. This theory also assumed that as spiritual ends were the highest human ends, the pope's jurisdiction was ultimately superior to that of secular rulers. The theory also assumed that the representatives of the two powers would cooperate in the work of achieving man's temporal and spiritual ends. The great conflict between church and state in the Middle Ages resulted from the fact that the precise boundaries of each sphere's jurisdiction remained blurred. It was Pope Innocent III whose decretals, especially *Venerabilem* and *Per venerabilem*, wrestled with the precise boundaries of the two jurisdictions. [32]

Innocent III exemplified his conception of the right order of the world at the Fourth Lateran Council in 1215. This great council brought together the leaders of church and state, bishops and abbots, representatives of kings and the Emperor, under the supervisory eye of the Pope. The theme of the Council was the harmonious cooperation of the two powers based on each jurisdiction recognizing its role in the larger scheme of things.

It was Innocent's theory of power and jurisdiction that underlay the sixteenth-and seventeenth-century Spanish conception of church-state relations and the theory on which the Spanish legitimized their conquest and possession of the Americas. However, this is not to say that Charles V or Philip II and their advisors understood Innocent's conception of church-state relations in the same way that the pope had done. Innocent III and his great successors saw the pope playing a strong, active role in the direction of Christian society. Innocent III, Innocent IV, and Boniface VIII, to identify only the most forceful of these popes, rejected any notion that the papal role was strictly limited to internal church matters. They took seriously the idea that the pope had the right, even the obligation, to guide secular rulers into the proper paths when necessary. The Spanish monarchs, however, reversed the emphasis, limiting the role of the pope to authorizing secular rulers to act in specific situations. Once the secular ruler has received papal authorization, the pope's role ended and he becomes a passive observer of events.

Spanish rulers did not deny that the pope could deprive them of their right to claim the Americas. Innocent's theory of papal power, as the Spanish understood it, did not deny to the pope that power. Indeed, the exquisite care with which the Spanish stated their case was designed to prevent them from being accused of heresy and thus lose the papal approbation they required to legitimate their possession of the Americas. For example, the Spanish refused to accept Hostiensis's theory that, with the coming of Christ, all lawful *dominium* belonged to those who were in the state of grace. If the Spanish thinkers had accepted that argument, opponents could have accused them of heresy, specifically Donatism. This ancient heresy, refuted by Augustine of Hippo (354-430), reappeared in the fourteenth and fifteenth centuries. [33] The Council of Constance condemned John Wyclif (c. 1330-1384) and John Hus (1372-1415) for, among other errors, holding the Donatist position on *dominium*. Spanish writers from Vitoria onward were careful to avoid any hint of Donatist teachings in their discussion of legitimate claims to the Americas. [34]

Perhaps, no one except the Spanish took seriously the assertion that papal universal jurisdiction enabled Alexander VI to grant the Americas to them. After all, some Catholic rulers rejected any such claims. As Francis I (1515-1547) of France observed before accepting the papal claim to grant newly discovered lands to the care of a particular Christian ruler, "he would like very much to see Adam's will to see how he divided up the world!" [35] At the same time, Francis I avoided direct confrontation with the Spanish in the Americas by encouraging the colonization of areas, such as Canada, that were not under effective Spanish control. [36] After all, a king of France who had obtained from the papacy the right of nominating candidates for all of the senior ecclesiastical positions within his kingdom, as Francis I had done by the terms of the Concordat of Bologna (1516), was in a poor position to doubt the extent of papal jurisdiction where spiritual matters were concerned. By the middle of the seventeenth century, even the Spanish came to accept the principle that "effective occupation" could provide "sufficient title" to the newly discovered lands, thus recognizing in practice some limitations on the extent of papal power and jurisdiction. [37]

In the final analysis, Spanish thinkers and royal officials did with the texts of the medieval theory of church-state relations what their contemporaries had done and were continuing to do with other ancient and medieval texts — they stretched and extended them in order to comprehend the circumstances found in the New World within a familiar intellectual framework. They found the three-centuries old dualist position on church-state relations quite adequate for justifying their position in the Americas simply by emphasizing the active role of the secular power acting at the request of and with the permission of the papacy. Unlike their imperial predecessors of the eleventh and twelfth centuries, the Spanish monarchs required no theory of the divine origin of their power to counter papal assertions of a superior jurisdiction. Solórzano, for example, identified the argument that God Himself had given responsibility for the inhabitants of the New World to the Spanish monarchs as one of the nine invalid arguments for Spanish control of the Americas. [38] There was no need to assert complete independence of the papacy and run the risk of being charged with heresy when the papacy authorized what the Spanish wanted in the first place. Given the religious and political situation within Europe, the papacy could not afford to alienate its strongest supporter, the Habsburg family. Having always asserted their interest in the spiritual work of converting the Indians to Christianity, the Habsburgs willingly assumed the role that the canonistic theory of church-state relations required of them. In a sense, because the circumstances were different, the Spanish monarchs of the sixteenth century achieved in practice a relationship with the papacy that would, no doubt, have satisfied the Hohenstaufen, had the German emperors been able to manipulate the papacy as the Hapsburgs were able to do. The debate about the legitimacy of the conquest of the Americas, in effect, also testified to the possibility that the papal theory of the two powers could be turned to the advantage of the secular power under some circumstances.

What Spanish legal theorists did with regard to the medieval theory of the two swords is simply another illustration of the way in which medieval ideas, practices, and institutions provided the foundations of at least two centuries of European overseas expansion. The assumption, a reasonable assumption at the time, was that the historical experience of Europeans with those outside of Europe was directly applicable to the peoples of the New World. Contrary to popular opinion in the twentieth century, sixteenth-century Europeans did not believe that the peoples of the New World were sub-or non-human. They did not, as Henry Steele Commager once wrote, have "no compunction about killing Indians because the Indians had no souls." [39] Quite the reverse, the Spanish assumed that the Aztecs, the Incas, and the other peoples whom they encountered were essentially just like themselves, that is descendants of Adam and Eve. From that assumption, they moved to another, namely that, because Indians were biologically just like themselves, they must also evolve politically and socially just as Europeans had done. Just as it took the first wave of explorers almost a generation to realize that they had not reached Asia, so too it took a long time for Europeans to recognize that, even if the Indians were biologically the same as themselves, this did not necessarily mean that they would or should follow the same path of social development. Europeans became aware only slowly of the "otherness" of the peoples of the New World. It took anywhere from one to two centuries.

Not until the beginning of the eighteenth century did Europeans become fully aware of the true "otherness" of the peoples whom they were encountering. Only with the development of modern biological theories that did not rely on the biblical account of man's origins was it possible to account for the differences in social and political evolution between Europe and the Americas in biological or racial terms. It took two centuries of dealing with the New World to become clear that the experience of medieval Europe was not immediately applicable.

We should not be surprised at the slow pace of change in European outlooks as a consequence of the discovery of the various new worlds following Columbus's first voyage. After all, medieval Europeans possessed a well-established world-view capable of comprehending all kinds of new experiences and placing them in their proper location within this all-embracing schema. The experience gained through contact with the New World only confirmed the essential correctness of the late-medieval world view — or so it seemed. The Europeans possessed the capacity to "save the appearances" by pulling, pushing, and twisting the evidence of their senses to fit their theories. In doing so, however, explorers and armchair theorists of exploration were doing exactly what a line of astronomers did in the wake of the publication of Copernicus's heliocentric theory. There is a period between acceptance of a new theory and the passing of an old one in which a variety of attempts are made to combine elements of the old and the new theories so that the old does not have to be completely rejected. As Thomas Kuhn has written, "[n]ormal science, for example, often suppresses fundamental novelties because they are necessarily subversive of its basic commitments." [40] It may well be that intellectuals and academics are by no means as enthusiastic about accepting new ideas as they like to think they are.

Two decades ago, John Elliott raised the question of why it took so long for Europeans to assimilate the experience of the New World and thus to affect the European outlook. [41] Scholars have responded to Elliott's question in a variety of ways. [42] Recently, surveying this literature, Anthony Grafton suggested an answer. The discoveries, he wrote, "had very little impact on European thought" because they "left European notions of history and civilization intact. They did not shake but confirmed European prejudices about the superiority of white Christians to those of other breeds and creeds." [43] While one might quarrel with one or another element of Grafton's opinion, his position is fundamentally correct. Rather to the surprise of many twentieth-century observers, the New World affected the Old World only slowly and not without struggle. That being the case, the medieval underpinnings of the early modern world deserve much fuller analysis than they have so far received because they remained the basis of the lives and outlook of Europeans well into the early modern era. What is even more deserving of attention is the way in which medieval ideas and institutions were extended and transformed in the course of being applied to the new circumstances that were emerging.

In the final analysis, the legacy of the quincentennial celebration of Columbus's first voyage will be a greater interest on the part of medievalists, whatever their disciplines, in ways in which the discovery of the New World affected the transformation of medieval ideas and institutions in the sixteenth and seventeenth centuries. This is not simply to engage in an academic turf war for space in the curriculum, but rather to deal with a problem rarely discussed yet of great significance, the way in which the medieval world was transformed into the modern world. Generally speaking, historians look at the fourth to eighth centuries as the period of great transformation, as the medieval world came into being. Of even greater and more immediate interest is the way in which the modern world emerged out of the medieval world. One might wish for a sympathetic Gibbon to write a history of the decline and fall of the medieval world, a history that would trace the transformation of medieval Europe through to the beginning of the eighteenth century, if not to August 4, 1789, when the French revolutionaries announced the end of the feudal regime. The end of the Middle Ages and the beginning of the modern world was a period of enormous transformation, the significance of which we are just coming to appreciate.

Notes

[1] B. Tierney, "Aristotle, Aquinas, and the Ideal Constitution," *Proceedings of the Patristic, Mediaeval, and Renaissance Conference* 4 (1979), 1-11.

[2] B. Tierney, "Natural Rights in the Thirteenth Century: A *Quaestio* of Henry of Ghent," *Speculum* 67 (1992), 58-68 at 68.

[3] There is a convenient collection of observations by contemporaries on the revival of true learning after the long dark night of the Middle Ages in *The Portable Renaissance Reader*, ed. J. Bruce Ross and M. Martin McLaughlin (New York 1953), 120-45.

[4] I employ the word "discovery" deliberately because it accurately describes the eventual impact of Columbus's first voyage on Europeans, namely the wonder and awe generated among Europeans when they came to realize that Columbus and those who followed him were revealing a world of which Europeans had not the slightest awareness previously.

[5] See for example: C. Verlinden, *The Beginnings of Modern Colonization*, trans. Y. Freccero (Ithaca 1970); F. Fernández-Armesto, *Before Columbus: Exploration and Colonization from the Mediterranean to the Atlantic, 1229-1492* (Philadelphia 1987); J.R.S. Phillips, *The Medieval Expansion of Europe* (Oxford 1988).

[6] C. Dawson, *The Making of Europe* (London 1932; reprint ed., New York 1956), 40-41; see also J. Muldoon, *The Expansion of Europe: The First Phase* (Philadelphia 1977).

[7] A.R. Lewis, "The Closing of the Mediaeval Frontier, 1250-1350," *Speculum* 33 (1958), 475-83; R. Bartlett, *The Making of Europe: Conquest, Colonization, & Cultural Change, 950-1350* (Princeton 1993).

[8] For example, see C.R. Boxer, *The Portuguese Seaborne Empire, 1415-1825* (New York 1969).

[9] C.R. Boxer, *The Church Militant and Iberian Expansion, 1440-1770* (Baltimore 1978), 78-79.

[10] G. Mattingly, *Renaissance Diplomacy* (Boston 1955), 283; see also J. Muldoon, "A Canonistic Contribution to the Formation of International Law," *The Jurist* 28 (1968), 265-79.

[11] Ibid., 284.

[12] On Scott, see J. Muldoon, "The Contribution of the Medieval Canon Lawyers to the Formation of International Law," *Traditio* 28 (1972), 483-97, esp. 488-89.

[13] A. Grafton, *New Worlds, Ancient Texts* (Cambridge 1992), 7.

[14] V.I.J. Flint, *The Imaginative Landscape of Christopher Columbus* (Princeton 1992), 116.

[15] J.H. Parry, *The Spanish Theory of Empire in the Sixteenth Century* (Cambridge 1940). Parry has provided a brief re-statement of his views in his J.H. Parry, *The Age of Reconnaissance* (New York 1963), 320-37. A recent article points out that Hostiensis did not originally hold this position and that his views on *dominium* were apparently a product of his reconsideration of the issues involved: see K. Pennington, Jr., "An Earlier Recension of Hostiensis's Lectura on the Decretals," *Bulletin of Medieval Canon Law* n.s. 17 (1987), 77-90.

[16] Parry, *Age of Reconnaissance*, 321.

[17] Ibid.

[18] For a brief introduction to the papacy's relations with Jews see: E.A. Synan, *The Popes and the Jews in the Middle Ages* (New York 1965); see also, J. Cohen, *The Friars and the Jews: The Evolution of Medieval Anti-Semitism* (Ithaca, NY 1982).

[19] On the development of this discussion, see J. Muldoon, *Popes, Lawyers and Infidels: The Church and the Non-Western World, 1250-1550* (Philadelphia 1979), 6-15.

[20] Parry, *Age of Reconnaissance*, 322.

[21] By the time that Parry was writing his work on the theory of empire, the brothers Carlyle had published their massive work on medieval political thought that demonstrated the wide range of medieval opinions on the nature and extent of papal and imperial power; See R.W. Carlyle and A.J. Carlyle, *History of Mediaeval Political Theory in the West* (Edinburgh and London 1903-1936), V,148-49, 359.

[22] F. de Victoria, *De Indis et de iure belli relectiones*, trans. J. Pawley Bate (Washington, DC 1917; reprint ed., New York 1964), 150. The most recent translation of Vitoria's work (which was not available to me) is F. de Vitoria, *Political Writings*, ed, A. Pagden and J. Lawrance (Cambridge 1991).

[23] J. Muldoon, "A Canonistic Contribution to the Formation of International law," *The Jurist* 28 (1968), 265-79.

[24] The most important discussions of that confrontation are to be found in the work of L. Hanke, *Aristotle and the American Indians: A Study in Race Prejudice in the Modern World* (Bloomington 1959) and *The Spanish Struggle for Justice in the Conquest of America* (Philadelphia 1949).

[25] Parry, *Age of Reconnaissance*, 332.

[26] On the importance of canonistic materials in the thought of Las Casas, see K.J. Pennington, Jr., "Bartolomé de Las Casas and the Tradition of Medieval Law," *Church History* 39 (1970), 149-61. For an appreciation of Pennington's work on Las Casas, see R. Adorno, "The Intellectual Life of Bartolomé de las Casas," The Andrew W. Mellon Lecturer, Tulane Univ., Fall 1992 (New Orleans 1992), 4.

[27] Ibid.

[28] The most convenient edition of the bulls involved is *European Treaties bearing on the History of the United States and its Dependencies to 1648*, ed., F.G. Davenport (Washington, DC 1917; reprint ed., Gloucester, MA 1967), 56-78.

[29] J. de Solórzano de Pereira, *De Indiarum Iure sive de iusta Indiarum Occidentalium Inquisitione, Acquisitione & Retentione* (Madrid 1777), I,ii,23 (title).

[30] Ibid., 1,2,c,23, para. 119-20. See also J. Muldoon, "Boniface VIII as Defender of Royal Power: *Unam Sanctam* as a Basis for the Spanish Conquest of the Americas," *Popes, Teachers, and Canon Law in the Middle Ages*, eds. J. Ross Sweeney and S. Chodorow, (Ithaca, NY 1989), 62-73.

[31] J. Muldoon, "Spiritual Conquests Compared: *Laudabiliter* and the Conquest of the Americas," *In Iure Veritas: Studies in Canon Law in Memory of Schafer Williams*, eds., S. Bowman and B. Cody (Cincinnati 1991), 174-86. Concerning the Irish response to *Laudabiliter*, see: J. Muldoon, "The Remonstrance of the Irish Princes and the Canon Law Tradition of the Just War," *American Journal of Legal History* 22 (1978), 309-25; and J.R.S. Phillips, "The Irish Remonstrance of 1317: An International Perspective," *Irish Historical Studies* 27 (1990), 112-29. In listing the medieval forerunners of *Inter caetera* and in stressing the long history of papal grants of people and lands to Christian rulers for the achievement of spiritual ends, Solórzano anticipated the work of a contemporary Mexican scholar who has argued that the papal claims contained in Alexander VI's bull derive from the Donation of Constantine: see L. Weckmann, *Las Bulas Alejandrinas de 1493 y la Teoriá Política del Papado Medieval* (Mexico City 1949).

[32] B. Tierney, " 'Tria Quippe Distinguit Iudicia . . .' A Note on Innocent III's Decretal *Per venerabilem*," *Speculum* 37 (1962), 48-59. The most extensive study of Innocent III's political views is F. Kempf, *Papsttum und Kaisertum bei Innocenz III.*

Die geistiaen und rechtlichen Grundlagen seiner Thronstreitpolitik, Miscellanea Historia Pontificiae 19 (Rome 1954).

[33] H.A. Deane, *The Political and Social Ideas of St. Augustine* (New York 1963), 34-35, 175-97.

[34] Vitoria, *De Indis*, 121: see also J. Muldoon, "John Wyclif and the Rights of the Infidels: The *Requerimiento* Re-examined," *The Americas* 36 (1980), 301-16.

[35] S. Eliot Morison, *The European Discovery of America: The Northern Voyages* (New York 1971), 435.

[36] French Huguenots, however, who obviously rejected *Inter caetera* in its entirety did attempt to settle in Brazil and Florida: see F. Parkman, *Pioneers of France in the New World* (Boston 1925), 26-181.

[37] J. Elliott, *The Old World and the New, 1492-1650* (Cambridge 1970), 101.

[38] Solórzano, 1,2,3.

[39] H. Steele Commager, "Should the Historian Make Moral Judgments," *American Heritage* 17, No. 2 (1966), 27, 87-93 at 91.

[40] T. Kuhn, *The Structure of Scientific Revolutions*, International Encyclopedia of Unified Science (Chicago 1970), II,2, 5.

[41] Elliott, *The Old World and the New*, 28.

[42] See, for example, M.T. Ryan, "Assimilating New Worlds in the Sixteenth and Seventeenth centuries," *Comparative Studies in Society and History* 23 (1981), 519-38.

[43] Grafton, 6.

Biological and Ecological Repercussions

of the Opening of the Oceans

after 1492

William H. McNeill

This Conference embraces an enormous range of themes across some fifteen centuries, but what I propose to talk about this morning exceeds even those capacious boundaries, since the opening of the oceans to European shipping occurred just before and after 1500, when the Renaissance was already old; and its consequences reverberate among us still — not least in the biological and ecological realms. But the organizers chose to devote both plenary sessions of this Eighteenth International Conference on Patristic, Medieval and Renaissance Studies to trans-Atlantic topics, and my assignment is to outline what historians have been learning about the biological and ecological consequences of the encounter between the Old world and the New that began in 1492.

This is a new focus of historical enquiry. Fifty years ago historians paid no attention to the non-human forms of life that crossed the oceans with the Conquistadores; and I know of only one scholar, an isolated museum staff member named Berthold Laufer, who, in the 1930s, proposed to study the counter-flow of American food crops to the Old World. Laufer prepared a booklet about potatoes, but, since it appeared as an obscure serial publication of the Field Museum of Natural History, [1] historians paid no attention. Consequently, when in the 1960s, William Langer, a famous Harvard professor, realized how the spread of potatoes had sustained the growth of population in nineteenth century Europe, he felt that he had made an important discovery, worthy of a lead article in the *American Historical Review*. [2]

As far as the historical profession was concerned, however, a more general understanding of the significance of the biological transformations that accompanied the opening of the oceans waited until the 1970s, when Alfred Crosby's seminal book, *The Columbian Exchange* (1972) and my *Plagues and Peoples* (1976) came out. Crosby followed up his initial venture into ecological history with *Biological Imperialism*

(1986), a global account of how innumerable Eurasian organisms —
crops, domestic animals, diseases, weeds, pests, insects and miscella-
neous other unintended hitch-hikers on European ships — altered
older ecological relations by invading previously insulated landscapes
after 1492.

Painstaking demographic studies of sixteenth and seventeenth century Mexico by Shelburne F. Cooke and Woodrow Wilson Borah paved
the way for sympathetic reception of this dawning ecological understanding, for Cook and Borah discovered far more drastic depopulation
than anyone had expected. [3] When their numerical results began to
come out, no plausible explanation of Amerindian die-off could be
found. Spanish cruelty, real though it sometimes may been, could not
account for the wholesale destruction of the work force Spaniards
wished to coerce. Only when historians came to recognize the racial
difference between a disease-experienced populations such as that inha-
biting Eurasia and Africa in 1500, and epidemiologically vulnerable,
disease-inexperienced peoples, like those of America, did the sad fate
of pre-Columbian inhabitants of the New World become intelligible.
Thereupon, a new understanding of the biological basis of the modern
European expansion around the entire globe dawned upon the historical profession. Crosby's Ecological Imperialism explored this new angle
of vision with admirable bravura. Paraphrase and summation of what
he had to say will constitute the main burden of my remarks this morning.

* * * * *

First, though, a look backward. What happened after the establishment of regular contacts across the oceans of the earth exposed larger
populations than ever before — both human and non-human — to
biological onslaught from afar. But invasion of new territory by especially successful organisms was exactly how biological evolution had
always proceeded. What was different after 1492 was the critical role
played by human beings, who built the ships and then utilized winds and
currents to cross previously insulating oceanic distances, and thus made
every hospitable shore into a theater for radically new biological as well
as cultural encounters.

To be sure, human intervention in ecological balances began long
before Columbus, when our paleolithic ancestors learned to use fire to
burn off dry vegetation, thus provoking new growth to feed the herds
they hunted. Agriculture and urbanism greatly extended human impact
on other forms of life. Indeed, its is probably true that ever since the
development of agriculture human beings have been the principal dis-
turbers of ecological balances throughout the earth; and we remain so

today and for the foreseeable future.

Some changes were deliberate and conscious. Selection of seed for crops and of animals for domestic production accorded with human purposes Across the centuries, these activities produced radically different creatures, as any visitor to a dog show or agricultural fair will recognize. Other changes were unintended and often defeated human wishes. In particular, humanity's persistent effort to escape from infectious disease was never completely successful, but presented infectious organisms with an unending variety of new challenges to their survival. Consequently, insofar as prophylaxis against infectious was effective, human action hastened the pace of biological evolution among infectious organisms. This became dramatically evident after the discovery of antibiotics, which have now created a whole new generation of germs capable of resisting their chemical assault.

This sort of unintended interaction between human beings and the surrounding ecological system is age-old and probably was just as important, overall, as anything that we and our predecessors did deliberately to alter prevailing life forms. Let me revert briefly to the history of infectious diseases because that offers a particularly good illustration of the unintended dimension of human impact on the ecosystem. Because germs were too small for human eyes to see, until only a little more than a century ago, deliberate efforts to cope with infectious diseases rested on dubiously efficacious medical theories and customary practices. A sort of blind man's buff ensued, whereby doctors' cures did almost as much harm as good. Human survival depended on the accumulation of antibodies against prevailing infections through age-old processes of biological evolution. Deliberate action and customary practices always affected the incidence of disease, but had almost random effects before advances of scientific medicine in the nineteenth and twentieth centuries brought most infections under control.

The resulting natural history of infectious diseases can be plausibly reconstructed. When humans began to gather into cities, infections passed more easily from host to host, making cities much more unhealthy than the open countryside. Moreover, as population density increased in the Old World, various herd diseases successfully transferred themselves from animal populations to humankind. These infections — including such familiar childhood diseases as smallpox, measles, mumps, whooping cough — needed large host populations — up to half a million in modern times — because they generated life-long resistance among survivors and, accordingly, had to find an unending supply of susceptible new-borns to keep the chain of infection going. Outside Eurasia and Africa, in the Americas, Australia, and oceanic islands generally, human populations were not exposed to these herd diseases. either because they remained too few, or because they did not have domesticated herd animals from which to contract them. Many other, less readily communicable diseases that were rife in Eurasia and Africa also failed to establish themselves among small islanded populations.

But, ironically, their previous good health made such isolated populations liable to sudden disaster whenever contact with disease-experienced peoples of Eurasia and Africa exposed them to new and lethal infections. Their bloodstreams lacked the complex array of antibodies that gave disease-experienced peoples inherited and acquired resistance to infections. The result was drastic and abrupt depopulation of both American continents, and an eventual re-population largely by descendants of Europeans and Africans. Similar disaster struck other previously isolated peoples in Australia, Oceania and, eventually, also in the Arctic north of both Siberia and Canada. The opening of the oceans, therefore, (and the subsequent penetration of Arctic lands) had the biological effect of creating a vast zone of demographic-disaster for human and others native forms of life. Wherever local ecosystems had previously flourished in isolation from the world's most highly evolved Eurasian-African complex, invasive organisms, arriving by ship, wrought havoc with the less highly evolved and therefore vulnerable local fauna and flora.

The biological gap that had opened across geologic ages between the two sides of the Atlantic remains, I venture to say, the most fundamental feature of American history across the past five hundred years. It explains, for instance, why the European discovery of America had such different consequences from anything provoked by European exploration of the coast of Africa which antedated (and led to) Columbus' fateful voyages.

From a biological point of view, the contrast between sub-Saharan Africa and America could not have been greater. Tropical Africa was the seat of the world's most tightly knit web of life. As far as humans were concerned, this manifested itself as a formidable array of tropical diseases, most of which could not survive freezing temperatures. Old World inhabitants of the temperate zone were thus safe from African diseases as long as they stayed home. On the other hand, African populations had to survive in the presence of particularly lethal forms of malaria, together with yellow fever, sleeping sickness, and a host of other infections that were unknown elsewhere. Outsiders, coming from Europe or Asia, nearly always succumbed after coming within range of the mosquitoes and other organisms that carried these lethal diseases, whereas inherited resistances and childhood inoculation allowed African populations to endure what strangers died of.

They therefore remained in firm possession of the land, even after European doctors learned how to minimize exposure to most tropical diseases, permitting a handful of European empire builders to extend

political control over nearly all of the continent by the end of the nineteenth century. But European rule in Africa came late, remained sup-
erficial, and disappeared soon after World War II. Among the newly
independent African states colonial boundaries, however arbitrary,
proveed to be surprisingly resilient., but within those boundaries diverse
African societies persist. Basic continuities with the pre-colonial past
therefore continue to give Africa a distinctive character of its own.

By contrast, within a few years of their initial lodgements, a handful of Europeans everywhere disrupted Amerindian society profoundly,
and the diseases they brought (together with profound demoralization)
often destroyed local populations entirely. Moreover, when labor short-
ages became acute, European entrepreneurs imported African slaves,
and, in due course, slave ships transferred some of Africa's most lethal
diseases to tropical America. Wherever European and African diseases
reinforced one another, Amerindian populations withered away.
Whites, too, even when exposed in infancy, were not as resistant to
malaria and yellow fever as blacks whose ancestors had, for untold generations, survived in the presence of these infections.

As a result, the population of many Caribbean islands and of the
tropical coastlands of central and south America is now predominantly
black, whereas in temperate climes, landscapes emptied by European
diseases were in due course re-populated primarily by descendants of
Europeans. But, as we all know, Africans and Amerindians, in varying
proportions, also played a part in the mingling of peoples — red,
white and black — that constitutes American society today. Asian
strands have entered the blend recently, and it seems almost certain
that the migration flows that reconstituted human society in the Americas so drastically after 1492 will persist as long as acute discrepancies of
living standards coexist with cheap transport and instant communica-
tion.

Perhaps I should pause to explain that disease differentials were
not the sole determinants of the population history of the Americas.
Social, economic, and political factors played a part too. So did currents of opinion and moral crusades, such as that which resulted in the
abolition of slavery in the nineteenth century. I pass these factors by
not because I think they were unimportant in affecting the geographical
distribution of, and all the other complex interrelationships among, the
diverse populations of post-Columbian America. I do so only because
my theme this morning is biological and ecological and since the disease
dimension of the post-Columbian history of devastating destruction
wrought by Old World infections on Amerindian peoples.

The same disproportion between local and Eurasian diseases
existed in Australia and in oceanic islands as well. The only explanation
for this phenomenon is so general as to be useless in explaining what

happened to particular species in the varying landscapes of newly con-
tacted lands. All one can say is that given a presumably uniform
frequency of genetic variation and subsequent selection, the larger landmass and resulting diversity of the Old World meant that evolution had
proceeded further in that part of the earth than elsewhere. As a result,
Eurasian and African life forms often prevailed over species as they had
evolved in other parts of the earth. But, as we shall soon see, from a
human point of view, some American food plants had enormous advantages, and, in due course, spread across much of the Old World.

* * * * *

So far I have focussed almost wholly on the way Old World dis-
ease-causing micro-organisms spread to new lands, both because I am
particularly familiar with the subject, and because they affected human
affairs more drastically and quickly than other biological changes. But
the complex symbiosis between disease organisms and human populations of the Old World that sustained the transplantation of European
and African populations to the New World after 1492 was only one
example of more general advantages that Old World fauna and flora
had when encountering the less developed biota of America and other,
previously isolated, landscapes.

Crosby's investigations turned up many examples of what happened when a plant or animal from the Old World got loose in a propitious environment, suddenly supplanting local species or reducing them
to marginality. In such cases, characteristically, some or all of the
checks that existed in the Old World to limit population growth were
temporarily removed. The intrusive organisms enjoyed a brief period
when their numbers were limited only or mainly by the rate of their
biological reproduction. This provoked sudden local population explo-
sions of a kind that are normally reserved for weed species that invade a
gash in the ecosystem created by some local disturbance — fire, flood,
or the like.

In all such situations, sooner or later new checks arise. Food supplies become scant, as happened for disease organisms when Amerindian bloodstreams developed antibodies against infection, and preda-
tors multiplied, as happened to vast herds of wild horses and cattle
when humans learned to live off them throughout the grasslands of
north and south America. To state matters more generally: local adap-
tations, together with subsequent arrival of various parasites and competing organisms from the Old World, soon checked the initial, lop-
sided multiplication of newly introduced species of animals and plants.
But anything like exact understanding of how ecological balances were
initially distorted and then gradually restored remains beyond our

knowledge.

Even today, mystery surrounds the way a new organism spreads across the country, as is now happening with the so-called "killer bees," and happened in my youth with English starlings, and what we called "trees of heaven" in Chicago in the 1930s. Exactly what allows the initial burst of numbers, and then begins to check and counterbalance the newcomer, until it fits more or less stably into a remodeled ecosystem, cannot be accurately measured. That is because the flows of matter and energy among biological species in the wild are enormously complex and incompletely understood. Suffice it to say, that a successful newcomer usually blooms like a weed, multiplies extravagantly, and then is cut back and becomes less conspicuous, less dominant, as it gets fitted into the ongoing balance of nature by dint of innumerable local adjustments on the part of all the organisms affected.

This, in general, is what happened to the forms of life (including human life) that were introduced to the Americas by European ships after 1492. The resulting balances, as they exist around us today, are very different from what prevailed before ships began to carry living things across the oceans. Just as the human population of the Americas blends red, white, and black, so, also, the fauna and flora around us combine Old and New World species in a continually evolving mix. Cross-breeding further complicates the balance among competing organisms. Experts cannot always be sure where a particular species originated, much less reconstruct the ebb and flow of different life forms that constituted the American biosphere at different times in the past.

Still two general observations seem worth making. In many instances, Old World species proved capable of displacing similar life forms partly because they were attuned to existence in one another's presence. For example, European grasses survived the hooves and teeth of horses, cattle, sheep (and buffaloes) more successfully than native American grasses could do; and this was, presumably, a factor in allowing them to displace native species from suitably mild and well-waters landscapes like that of Kentucky. At any rate, a European immigrant, the famous blue grass, was on the ground to greet Daniel Boone, though no one knows when or how that particular plant crossed the mountains and began to thrive on Kentucky's limestone soils.

This rather surprising fact also illustrates a second general principle: ecological impact frequently outran European observation. The wilderness penetrated by pioneer hunters, trappers, and settlers was not "the forest primeval" as Longfellow and other nineteenth century Americans supposed. Shocks, arising from the arrival of new forms of life from the Old World, had already altered older ecological relationships in greater or lesser degree before Europeans arrived on the scene, and, of course, surviving records, that allow us to know anything about local fauna and flora, usually lagged well behind the arrival of the first white men. Perhaps, someday, if pollen analysis at enough archaeological sites can be precisely dated and compared, researchers may learn more about what happened; but, as far as I know, this remains a possibility for the future that has not yet been widely exploited.

* * * * *

Changes wrought by deliberate human action are somewhat easier to follow. Here the dominant fact was that European settlers brought with them the crops and domestic animals they were accustomed to at home, and sought simply to transplant them onto new ground. By and large, they succeeded in the temperate zones of north and south America where soil and weather conditions resembled those of Europe. In particular, the array of domestic animals familiar in Europe allowed settlers to establish a pattern of farming that differed fundamentally from what Amerindians had developed before them. Plows instead of digging sticks, cleared fields instead of slash and burn cultivation, wheeled transport instead of human portage, woolen cloth instead of skin and bark clothing, a diet in which dairy products supplemented meat: all these depended on the availability of horse, sheep, and cattle. The net effect was a more productive agriculture, capable of sustaining larger populations than had previously existed in the temperate forests of north and south America.

On the other hand, Spanish and Portuguese efforts to reproduce familiar forms of cultivation in Mexico and Peru (and in the tropical lowlands of America) were largely unsuccessful. Wheat and other European staples did not thrive in the heartlands of the Spanish empire, and the disruption of labor-intensive forms of cultivation provoked by initial disease disasters and subsequent social disorganization after the conquest meant that far less intensive forms of land use came to prevail. Thus, for example, Mexican cattle ranching, as it emerged during the seventeenth century, supported far fewer people than before. Sufficient labor to sustain older, intensive forms of cultivation had become unavailable, and the skills involved were therefore forgotten.

On the other hand, Dutch, British, French, and Portuguese entrepreneurs established a radically new form of agriculture — the sugar plantation — in tropical lowlands of South America and the Caribbean islands. Worked by gangs of African slaves, this quasi-industrial form of agriculture had existed on a small scale on some Mediterranean and Atlantic islands before taking root in the New World. But the scale of plantation agriculture increased enormously after 1600, when the ready availability of slaves, of land and everything else needed for raising, refining, and marketing sugar, together with an all but insatiable European sweet tooth, made sugar plantations in the New World extremely profitable.

The resulting sugar boom resembled the sudden explosion of newly introduced species on American soil, for spreading sugar plantations created an industrialized monoculture that aimed at displacing all other forms of plant life from wide swathes of tropical lowland in Brazil and the Caribbean. Then, in the nineteenth century, the boom faded. Soil exhaustion, abolition of the African slave trade, and the cultivation of sugar beets in Europe combined to depress the sugar trade, and when slavery itself was abolished (between 1833 and 1888), liberated slaves were left to pursue subsistence as best they could in ravaged, though sometimes still beautiful, landscapes.

The plantation regime of the American tropics was unique as well as transitory. But even in regions where European styles of cultivation turned out to be generally successful, exact adherence to Old World practices proved to be impractical. The story taught to me in school about Squanto, the friendly Indian who taught the Pilgrims to plant corn by putting four kernels in each hill and fertilizing it with a fish, buried head down, illustrates how quickly English settlers learned new ways to farm in the American environment.

Incidentally, the fact that Squanto could lead the Pilgrims onto ready-made fields in order to demonstrate the proper technique for raising corn — a fact not remarked upon by my school book — was possible only because a devastating epidemic had come up the coast (presumably from Jamestown) a few years before the Pilgrims landed, and destroyed so many of the local inhabitants that the uncultivated fields awaited the newcomers. Since such epidemics commonly outran face-to-face contacts white pioneers in North America regularly found emptied lands when they showed up, and blithely disregarded traces of older habitation, even when they were as conspicuous as cleared fields in the Massachusetts forest ought to have been!

When they tried to create new fields amid the forest for themselves, white settlers quickly discovered that the staples of Amerindian slash and burn cultivation in North America — corn, squash, and beans — were much better suited to pioneering in wooded landscapes than wheat or any other European crop. As a result, wheat lost the primacy it enjoyed in Europe. Instead, maize took over. Only after stumps had decayed so that plowing became possible, could wheat and other European grains be cultivated successfully. Colonists continued to prefer wheat bread; but few could afford it. Corn meal, being far cheaper and more abundant, provided the basic calories upon which colonial society depended. Ere long, English-speaking Americans transferred the word "corn" from wheat to maize, creating a linguistic confusion that survives to the present and still attests the importance of this substitution.

Then, beginning in the 1840s but reaching full flower only after the Civil War, a radially new style of mechanized agriculture evolved in the United States. Heavy plows and mechanical reapers allowed the conversion of Middle Western prairies into vast new wheat fields, and corn was demoted to the status of animal feed. The high protein diet, featuring meat and dairy products, to which we are now accustomed actually turned wheat bread, which had been a luxury, into a modest supplement to meat and potatoes.

But since potatoes, too, originated in America, this alteration in our food habits did not escape direct dependence on New World crops; and, long before American agriculture assumed its existing format, the truly remarkable attractions of maize, potatoes and some other American crops, spread them across the Old World, beginning on a large scale, in the second half of the seventeenth century. The American crop migration between, roughly 1600 and 1900, constituted a very considerable alteration in the ecology of the Old World, and I propose to devote what time remains to this theme.

* * * * *

First of all, we should ask what was it about corn, potatoes, peanuts, tomatoes, and sweet potatoes — to name the most important of the crops that spread across the ocean from America — that made them preferable to other cultivated plants? The simple answer is that in suitable soils and climates, they produced larger yields per acre than anything else. I know of no explanation for this phenomenon; but if one compares the number of seeds on stalk of wheat with kernels on an ear of corn, the difference will become obvious. Moreover, a single corn stalk produces several ears. This means that seed-to-harvest ratios are enormously larger for corn than for wheat or any other European grain. Correspondingly, less of the harvest has to be saved for seed; more can be consumed; and far, far more can be produced on a given amount of land. These are enormous tangible advantages and explain why corn spread as widely as its did in Europe, Africa, and Asia. Potatoes, too, produce far more calories per acre than grain does in the cool climate of northwestern Europe, and in China sweet potatoes thrive on mountain slopes where rice paddies can not be constructed. Peanuts and tomatoes also yield abundantly in propitious soils and climates; and often supplement local diets that once were short of the vitamins and proteins they now provide.

To be sure, there were disadvantages. Maize lacks some of the amino acids required for human nutrition. Thus a diet of nothing but corn provokes a debilitating deficiency disease known as pellagra. On the other hand, potatoes come close to providing a balanced diet for humans, but they cannot be easily stored for long periods of time, as grain can be, making it hard to guard against crop failure by carrying stocks over from year to year. (In Peru, the Incas preserved great vast quantities of potatoes in official storehouses by freezing them; but this technique never spread beyond the *Altiplano*.)

A more important drawback to the spread of the American food crops was that they required rainfall throughout the growing season, whereas wheat and other grains ripened best under drought conditions. As a result, maize needed more summer rain than most of Europe's Mediterranean lands enjoyed as well as warmer temperatures than prevailed in trans-Alpine countries. Hence, it could only thrive in a few parts of Europe, most notably in the Po valley of northern Italy, and in the northern Balkans. Similarly in Africa, everywhere north of the Equator, undependable rainfall made maize growing risky; and its vulnerability to locusts was another serious handicap. By comparison, drought during part of the growing season did not do much damage to the old staple, millet; while root crops, like manioc, regenerates after a locust attack while maize cannot. As a result, only in the southern parts of Africa, where rainfall was more abundant and locusts fewer, did African peoples find it possible to enjoy the superior productivity of maize.

Climates and soils in Asia varied enormously and we know very little about how American food crops found lodgement in that continent. Recent agricultural statistics show that China has been by far the most hospitable country. Sweet potatoes flourished early on, especially in the south; but maize, potatoes, and peanuts also became important crops, supplementing rather than displacing the older staples of rice and wheat. The massive growth of Chinese population since about 1650 depended directly on the extra food these crops provided. In India and the Middle East, rainfall and temperature do not fit the needs of American crops nearly so well, and they never became very important. By contrast, the vast plain, extending eastward into Siberia from the Low countries through Germany, Poland, and Russia, was well suited to potatoes. Accordingly, the political and economic consequences that flowed from the spread of potatoes across this vast expanse of fertile soil, with correspondingly vast increases in food production, was the most important alteration in human affairs provoked by American food crops in the Old World.

A third drawback to maize, potatoes and the other American crops was that repeated hoeing was required to keep down weeds; whereas grains did not need to be cultivated because they sprang up quickly enough to crowd out competing plants. Among the major Old World crops, only rice (which had to be transplanted from seed beds into the shallow water of specially prepared paddies) demanded anything like the amount of field labor that the American crops required; and perhaps it is not accidental that rice was also the only Old World crop whose caloric yield per acre matched or exceeded what American crops could produce.

The extra labor required for raising corn, potatoes, and the other American food crops, together with the normal prejudice against accepting a new food staple, prevented their initial acceptance in Europe as more than botanical curiosities. Only when some unusual emergency upset old routines, or when population growth began to press against the limits of local food supplies, while simultaneously creating an underemployed rural work force, could the American food crops come into their own. We know something about how this happened in Europe; but for the rest of the Old World the necessary historical research has barely begun.

Let me, therefore, conclude by sketching what we know about three important European cases: maize in the Balkans, potatoes in Ireland, and potatoes in the north European plain.

Maize arrived in the Balkans in the seventeenth century, and Christian subjects of the Ottoman empire quickly learned to exploit it in three different environments. One was in mountain valleys of the western Balkans, where summer encampments for shepherds were converted into year round villages when maize fields proved capable of providing sufficient cereal foods to supplement what the flocks produced. These villages escaped malaria, which was a serious health hazard in the plains; and Ottoman authorities usually did not even try to tax them. Under these favorable conditions, population grew rapidly and by the last decades of the eighteenth century was pressing hard against local subsistence. Young men, accordingly started to reverse the old shepherds' summer migration from plains to the hills by descending from their overcrowded villages to work as hired hands or as construction laborers in town. And when peaceable employment could not be found, these same young men took to arms and became bandits. The fighting manpower of the Greek revolution (1821-1828) derived mainly from such bands; and thereafter guerrilla became endemic in Greece and the rest of the western Balkans.

Since the late eighteenth century, therefore, the political and military history of the western Balkans turned on whether the surplus manpower of food-deficit villages in the mountains found peaceable employment in the plains or instead resorted to getting the food they needed by force of arms. I need scarcely remind you that armed insurrection still thrives in those parts, as recent events in Bosnia prove. Without maize and the permanent occupation of mountain valleys that it permitted, the history of that part of Europe would have been entirely different. Indeed, since World War I was sparked in Bosnia, one might argue that the history of the world was deflected from its course by the repercussions of this rather obscure and little known ecological transformation.

The second Balkan environment where maize played a central role was in the forested plain of Shumadia, south of Belgrad. Here, beginning in the late seventeenth century, Serbian pioneers penetrated dense, uninhabited forest, relying on maize and pigs in exactly the same way that American pioneers were then doing in the Appalachian piedmont. Like mountain villagers to the south and west of them, these Serb pioneers, secluded in forest clearings, escaped Ottoman taxation for the long time; and, in 1803, when the Turkish authorities in Belgrad tried to collect taxes from a population that by then had occupied most of Shumadia, they provoked revolt. This Balkan echo of our national history led, eventually, to the emergence of an independent Serbian state. Subsequently, Serbian ex-frontiersmen remained notoriously unruly and aggressive, as generations of European diplomats discovered to their dismay, and as we are doing again in 1993. Serbs thus reproduced *in parvo* a European version of the American frontier experience, relying on maize, just as Americans did, and remaking their corner of the world by doing so.

Maize played a very different, yet decisive, role in a third Balkan region, the plains of Rumania. Unlike the situation in the western Balkans and in Shumadia, when maize arrived in Rumania in the mid-seventeenth century the Ottoman empire exercised very effective, though indirect, economic and political control. Landowners ruled over peasant serfs, requiring them to produce wheat and meat for sale in Constantinople. The peasants depended on subsistence plots of maize, and for a long time, since their social superiors had no use for the strange new cereal, their numbers multiplied on the strength of the new crop's extraordinary productivity. By the nineteenth century, however, too many Rumanian peasants were eating nothing but maize, with the result that pelagra became endemic. Thus in 1858, when the by-play of European diplomacy made Rumania an independent state, a dispirited, poverty-stricken rural population found itself profoundly alienated from its rulers, most of whom were absentee landlords. Despite numerous and complicated subsequent upheavals, Rumanian society still exhibits the unusually wide gap between government and people that the combination of commercial export agriculture with subsistence maize cultivation created.

Oddly enough, the coexistence of commercial with subsistence agriculture that characterized Rumanian society and economy after 1650, was duplicated in Ireland, with the difference that potatoes rather than maize were the American crop that fitted the moist, cool Irish climate. Ireland, in fact, was the first European country where potatoes came to provide the principal food for a majority of the population; and did so because of the catastrophe that disrupted older ways of life when, in 1649-1652, Cromwell's armies, fresh from their victories in England, defeated the Irish and decided to confine the surviving Catholic population to the barren province of Connaught. But as it happened, Basque fishermen from Spain had already introduced potatoes to Connaught, where, with simple spade cultivation, a single acre of potatoes could support an entire family and nourish it well if supplemented by a little milk.

Once the Irish discovered the possibility of living so cheaply, they speedily undercut the English settlers that Cromwell had planted in the rest of Ireland. Irishmen who only needed an acre for potatoes and pasture rights for a cow could afford to pay higher rents and work for lower wages than English laborers who insisted on eating bread in a land where wheat did not flourish owing to excessive moisture. Accordingly, Cromwell's plan to settle Ireland with Protestants failed because Protestant landlords hired potato-eating Catholics to produce beef and other commodities for sale in England, thus making their estates profitable.

Ireland's subsequent history turned on this fact, and when, in the 1840s, bigger, faster steam ships carried a parasitic fungus from Peru to Irish potato fields, one of the great disasters of the nineteenth century ensued. The newly introduced fungus ruined potato fields throughout Ireland (and in other parts of Europe too). Resulting crop failure faced millions of the rural Irish with starvation. Those who survived undertook to change their ways, either by emigrating (and thereby altering the ethnic mix in America, Australia, and other places overseas), or by pulling themselves up by their bootstraps, partly by postponing marriage until enough land to support a new family with more than potatoes was somehow available and partly by mounting a sustained and eventually successful political assault against their Protestant landlords. So just as the history of the Balkans since about 1650 depended on the role of maize in those parts, so also the unique dynamic of Irish history in the same period of time turned upon the way potatoes preserved and then, with the famine, transformed Irish society, economy and cultural-political life.

Finally, a few words about the main theater of action for American food crops in the Old World, i.e., the spread of potatoes across the north European plain. Two circumstances made the spread of potatoes particularly rewarding in that environment. First, in time of war peasants could assure themselves of a food supply simply by leaving their potatoes in the ground and digging them as needed throughout the winter. Grain, in contrast, had to be gathered into barns where soldiers could requisition it, leaving the producers to starve. In Belgium, Walloons and Flemings discovered this simple form of insurance against military requisitioning during the War of the Spanish Succession, 1700-1713. Half a century later, during the Seven Years War, 1756-17633, Frederick the Great made it government policy to propagate potatoes in Prussia when he realized how effectively they could preserve the peasantry who provided the recruits and tax income he needed for his army. Then after another half century, the wars of the French revolution (1792-1815) carried the tuber into Russia, where it had the same tonic effect on the Tsar's capability of mobilizing his subjects for war.

Aside from strengthening governments and preserving tax payers by blunting the rages of famine and disease in wartime, potatoes also sustained a prolonged and hitherto unparalleled population growth that set in across the entire north European plain after about 1750. Potatoes could do this because they increased calorie yields enormously. To begin with, when planted on fallow fields, they did not reduce grain production in the slightest. The purpose of fallowing was to allow the elimination of weeds by plowing them under in summer, before they could produce seeds. But hoeing potatoes killed weeds more laboriously but just as effectively as summer plowing could do; and provided a new and abundant human food into the bargain. Such serendipity magnified the rewards of potato cultivation enormously. Total calorie production could be multiplied by something like four times simply by eliminating fallow and fitting potatoes into the crop rotation. Extra hands were needed for hoeing; but population growth took care of that.

By the 1840s, potatoes had become important enough in northern Europe to make the potato blight into a subsistence crisis for the poor, especially in Belgium and western Germany. But nothing as catastrophic as the Irish famine ensued because nowhere on the continent did a rural population depend entirely on potatoes. Sprays and resistant strains were soon introduced to counteract the fungus, and potatoes quickly became a staple food for all the inhabitants of the north European plain, from the Low Countries to the Urals and beyond.

The major consequence was the rise of Germany in the second half of the nineteenth century, for without the enormously expanded food base that potatoes provided, Germany could not have fed its rapidly growing population nor become the great industrial power it was in 1914. And without its potato fields, Germany could not have waged the two world wars of this century. In short, without potato fields to feed the vastly increased population of northern Europe, the whole shape of world affairs would have followed a different course.

* * * * *

These examples from European history could be replicated in other parts of the Old World, though in most places exact knowledge of the impact of American food crops (not to mention other life forms imported from America) is still scrappy or entirely absent, [4] But despite the gaps in our information — and they are enormous — we may be sure that the world is still resonating to the extraordinary ecological and demographic disturbances precipitated by the opening of the oceans. Nothing like stability has yet been attained, and it is unlikely to arise as long as human capacity to intervene in natural processes continues to enlarge.

To be sure, complete ecological stability never existed, so the modern experience differs only in the pace and scale from what happened locally in older times. What was new in 1492 was that biological encounters became global, and now, towards the close of the twentieth century, historians are beginning to understand how powerfully and pervasively the resulting changes in the ecosystem — some deliberate, some unintended — affected the entire social, economical, political, and cultural spectrum of human affairs. I submit that this constitutes a notable enlargement of understanding, offering one more dimension to bear in mind when contemplating the mystery and wonder of our past, present, and future on this earth.

Notes

[1] Berthold Laufer, *The American Plant Migration; I: The Potato*, Field Museum, Anthropological Series, No. 418, (Chicago 1938).

[2] William T. Langer, "Europe's Initial Population Explosion," *American Historical Review* 69 (1963), 1-17.

[3] Cook began publishing articles on Mexican population in the 1930s, but the definitive summation of numerous local parish studies appeared as Shelburne F. Cook and Woodrow Borah, *Essays in Population History: Mexico and the Caribbean*, 2 vols. (Berkeley 1971-73). The high estimates for pre-Columbian population that Cook and Borah came up with have since been challenged; but no one doubts today that catastrophic die-off occurred between 1521 and about 1650, when the nadir for Indian populations of central Mexico was attained. In places further removed from the centers of Spanish activity, disease exposures were delayed and local population disaster came later. The process has not yet ended. Drastic disease die-offs in remoter parts of northern Canada were still in progress in the 1950s. See Farley Mowat, *The Desperate People* (Boston 1959). And the same epidemiological destruction is still occurring in the Brazilian rain forest.

[4] Herman J. Viola and Carolyn Margolis, eds., *Seeds of Change* (Washington and London 1991), 43-59, with bibliographical note on 264, provides recent survey of what is known about the career of American food crops in the Old World.

Index of Names